DELEGATES DEBATE AT CONSTITUTIONAL CONVENTION—1787

Painting by Alton S. Tobey

My debt to history is one which
cannot be calculated. I know of no other
motivation which so accounts for my
awakening interest as a young lad in the
principles of leadership and government. . . .
I know that the one great external influence
which, more than anything else,
nourished and sustained that interest in
government and public service was the endless
reading of history which I began as a boy
and which I have kept up ever since.

HARRY TRUMAN

The unparalleled rise of America
has not been the result of riches in lands,
forests, or mines; it sprang from
the ideas and ideals which liberated minds
and stimulated the spirits of men.
In those ideas and ideals are the soul
of the people. No American can
review this vast pageant of progress without
confidence and faith, without courage, strength,
and resolution for the future.

HERBERT HOOVER

Kennedy: "A Nation of Immigrants," New York, 1959
Eisenhower: Reader's Digest, October, 1948
Truman: "Memoirs," © 1955, Time Inc.
Hoover: 150th anniversary address, Yorktown, Va., October 19, 1931

Important Dates and Events to Remember
〜 1783-1850 〜

1783 September, Britain signs peace terms and the Revolution formally ends.

1786 September, Shays' Rebellion. Hard times after Revolution cause farmers' uprising in Massachusetts.

1787 May 25, Constitutional Convention opens in Philadelphia, Pennsylvania. September 17, Constitution is signed by 39 of 42 delegates at convention.

1788 June 21, New Hampshire is 9th state to ratify Constitution. It becomes supreme law of the land.

1789 April 6, George Washington is elected first President of the United States; John Adams is Vice-President.
September 25, Congress accepts "Bill of Rights." It becomes the Constitution's first 10 amendments (December 15, 1791).

1791 March 4, Vermont becomes 14th state. December 12, urged by Alexander Hamilton, Bank of the United States opens in Philadelphia.

1792 June 1, Kentucky becomes 15th state. December 5, Washington and Adams are re-elected President and Vice-President.

1793 Eli Whitney invents cotton gin.

1794 August 20, army of General Anthony Wayne defeats Indians at Fallen Timbers in Ohio Territory.

1796 December 7, John Adams is President; Thomas Jefferson Vice-President.

1799 December 14, George Washington dies at Mount Vernon, Virginia.

1800 December 3, tie sends presidential election to House of Representatives.

1801 February 17, House votes Jefferson President, Aaron Burr Vice-President. May 14, demanding more tribute money from American ships sailing the Barbary Coast, Pasha of Tripoli declares war on United States.

1803 April 30, United States buys Louisiana Territory from France for $15,000,000.

1804 Meriwether Lewis and William Clark begin 2-year exploration of Northwest. July, Burr kills Alexander Hamilton in duel at Weehawken, New Jersey.

1805 June 4, Barbary Wars end. Pasha of Tripoli accepts peace without tribute.

1807 August 17, Robert Fulton's steamboat, *Clermont*, makes first trip up the Hudson River from New York to Albany.

1808 December 7, James Madison is elected President.

1811 November 7, General William Henry Harrison defeats Indians at Tippecanoe Creek (Indiana).

1812 April 30, Louisiana becomes 18th state. June 19, provoked by British interference with American affairs, Congress declares war against Great Britain. August 12, General William Hull surrenders Detroit, Michigan, to British. December 2, Madison is re-elected.

1813 September 10, Captain Oliver Hazard Perry defeats British on Lake Erie.
September 30, Americans retake Detroit.
October 5, William Henry Harrison, pursuing British retreating from Detroit, catches and defeats them at Thames River, Ontario.

1814 August 24, British occupy Washington, burn Capitol and White House.
September 24, moved by American resistance at Fort McHenry, Maryland, Francis Scott Key writes *Star-Spangled Banner*.
December 24, peace treaty, ending War of 1812, is signed at Ghent, Belgium.

1815 January 8, unaware the war is over, Andrew Jackson's troops rout British at New Orleans, Louisiana.

1816 December 4, James Monroe is elected President.
December 11, Indiana is 19th state.

1817 December 10, Mississippi is admitted as 20th state.

1818 December 3, Illinois is 21st state.

1819 December 14, Alabama is 22nd state.

1820 February, attempting to end feud over admission of free and slave territories, Congress accepts Missouri Compromise.
March 15, Maine becomes 23rd state.

1821 August 10, Missouri is 24th state.

1823 December 2, Monroe Doctrine warns European powers against interference in New World politics.

1825 February 9, when neither John Quincy Adams nor Andrew Jackson receives enough electoral votes to win presidency, House decides in favor of Adams.
October 26, Erie Canal, running from Buffalo to Albany, New York, is completed.

1828 December 3, Jackson wins presidency.

1832 December 5, Jackson is re-elected.

1836 March 2, American settlers in Texas declare territory independent of Mexico.
March 6, Santa Anna defeats Americans at Alamo in Texas; all defenders die.
April 21, at San Jacinto, Texas, Sam Houston defeats Santa Anna decisively.
June 15, Arkansas becomes 25th state.
December 7, Martin Van Buren is elected 8th President of United States.

1837 January 26, Michigan is 26th state.

1840 December 2, William Henry Harrison becomes President.

1841 April 4, Harrison dies. Vice-President John Tyler succeeds him.

1844 December 4, James K. Polk is elected President.

1845 March 1, Congress annexes Texas. Decision angers Mexican government.
March 3, Florida becomes 27th state.
December 29, Texas is 28th state.

1846 April 25, Mexicans and Americans skirmish on Texas soil and Congress declares war on Mexico (May 13).
December 28, Iowa becomes 29th state.

1847 February 22, at Buena Vista, Mexico, Zachary Taylor defeats Santa Anna.
March 29, General Winfield Scott captures Vera Cruz, and then Mexico City (September 14).

1848 January 24, gold is discovered at Sutter's Mill, California. Gold rush begins.
February 2, Mexico signs peace treaty with United States.
November 7, Zachary Taylor is elected President.

1850 July 9, Taylor dies. Vice-President Millard Fillmore becomes President.

PREAMBLE TO
THE CONSTITUTION OF THE UNITED STATES

We the people of the United States, in order to form a more perfect Union, establish justice, insure domestic tranquility, provide for the common defense, promote the general welfare, and secure the blessings of liberty to ourselves and our posterity, do ordain and establish this Constitution for the United States of America.

THE GOLDEN BOOK

HISTORY
of the
UNITED STATES

by **EARL SCHENCK MIERS**
LITT. B., M.A., L.H.D.

**VOLUME
4
BUILDING THE
NATION**

Paintings by **ALTON S. TOBEY**

Drawings by **RICHARD P. KLUGA**

Technical Consultants:
L. ETHAN ELLIS AND RICHARD M. BROWN
of the Department of History, Rutgers University

HERBERT J. SANBORN, *Art Research*

GOLDEN PRESS **NEW YORK**

How To Use This Volume BUILDING THE NATION tells of the problems facing the new United States from 1783 to 1850. The book may be read from cover to cover. It discusses many events that took place over a long span of time. The events taken up in each chapter are described briefly at the opening of the chapter and also on the contents page. This will allow the reader to find any subject he wants quickly and easily. Each section of the text also has the dates of the period it covers printed in blue at the top of the page. The principal events and the dates on which they occurred are listed in the timetable on the inside front cover. Maps are included throughout the text, and also on the inside back cover. An index for the entire series is contained in Volume X.

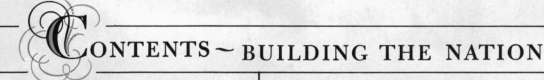

CONTENTS ~ BUILDING THE NATION

Library of Congress Catalog Card Number: 63-9433
© Copyright 1963 by Golden Press, Inc. and The Ridge Press, Inc.   Printed in the U.S.A. by Western Printing and Lithographing Co.

Designed and produced by
The Ridge Press, Inc.
551 Fifth Avenue, New York, N.Y.

A COUNTRY IN CHAOS

*America has won its independence,
but finds that its problems
are just beginning.*

The Revolution had ended. Now that the army was disbanded and a peace treaty with Britain signed, America settled down in 1783 to living with its newly won independence. After almost ten years of war, the people thought that life would now be easier. But peace, in its way, proved as difficult as war. Sometimes people wondered whether the liberty for which they had sacrificed so much had been worth the struggle.

Compared with nations like Great Britain and France, the infant United States seemed puny. In 1790 it had about 4,000,-000 inhabitants. They were so widely scattered that there were fewer than five persons to every square mile. With the exception of perhaps 12,000 pioneers who had made their homes beyond the Appalachian Mountains, the people inhabited a narrow strip of land along the Atlantic seacoast. Roads were few, poorly built, and often dangerous. Cities and towns were small. By the time news of Europe reached America, it was six weeks to three months out of date.

For the most part, the people thought only of their own affairs. Home was the center of their universe. A quarrel with a neighbor could easily become a family feud, a little war. Tories who had fled service in the army during the Revolution were not welcome on their return. Sometimes they were tarred and feathered and driven out of the neighborhood.

The trouble was that the country and its people were penniless. When the French and British troops left and the American forces were disbanded, the farmers lost a major market for their produce.

European merchants flooded America with the surpluses they had built up during the war, selling goods at sacrifice prices to some storekeepers. This cutthroat competition threatened to ruin many other American shopkeepers, who were loaded down with wartime surpluses of their own.

Britain now put heavy duties on Yankee ships that entered British ports, and Spain closed her ports in Europe and America to United States shipping. Without the protection of a strong navy, Yankee vessels sailing into the Mediterranean were forced to pay the Barbary pirates, who swarmed out of the ports of Tunis, Algeria, and Tripolitania on the North African coast.

States often acted more like enemies than partners. Pennsylvania and New York, more prosperous than their neighbors, passed laws to keep foreign goods from their ports. Little New Jersey and Connecticut, however, received such goods freely and closed their eyes to the smuggling that their citizens carried on with Pennsylvania and New

At the end of the Revolution, most Americans lived along the eastern seaboard.

POPULATION DENSITY
AT THE END
OF THE REVOLUTION

- - - Present state boundaries
• Major towns
Heavily populated areas
Sparsely settled areas

York. When, in return, New York placed a high tax on farm products from New Jersey, business suffered and the government was weakened by loss of income.

What "hard" money remained in America after the Revolution consisted of various foreign coins, and these were rapidly disappearing. People who owned land could not borrow money on it, for land was too plentiful. Paper money had little value and barter (trading goods) became common. To make matters worse, Congress had no power to raise taxes, regulate business, or place duties on imports. To gain that power Congress had to obtain the consent of all the states, a task that was impossible at the time.

Something had to give. Too many people were facing poverty and starvation or imprisonment for their debts. More and more people said: "Let the states print more paper money. Make it a law that such money must be accepted in payment of debts."

Paper money has value because something of *real* value—usually gold or silver—backs it up. Today you can take a paper dollar to the United States Treasury and get a dollar's worth of silver for it. If a country prints paper money without having gold or silver to back each dollar, that money becomes "cheaper." If there are five paper dollars in circulation and only one dollar's worth of silver in the Treasury, each paper dollar is really worth only twenty cents.

But in everyday business dealings—paying debts and buying goods—people have faith in their currency and a dollar remains a dollar. A $10 debt may be paid with ten one-dollar bills; nobody can say, "You now owe me $50 because the dollar has a *real* value of only twenty cents."

So in times of stress, people who owe money or can't afford to buy things want "cheap" money—more dollars. Those who are owed or who sell things want "hard" money, as close to a hundred-cent dollar as they can get.

In 1786 practically every state in the

Colonial money

281

Union was torn by this struggle over "cheap money." By that time, seven states were issuing more paper money. As a result, there was a flood of paper money that fell quickly in value.

TROUBLE OVER MONEY

In Rhode Island, where the farm vote had made paper money legal, warfare nearly broke out in communities like Providence and Newport. Here many shopkeepers who had paid hard money for their goods refused to sell them for cheap money. Farmers refused to ship their produce into these towns, hoping to starve out the oppo-

sition. Shops closed. Skulls were cracked and noses bloodied in street fights. When the court upheld the right of a butcher to refuse to sell meat for paper money, the people's anger turned on the judges. Almost all judges who decided cases in favor of the merchants lost their jobs.

Massachusetts voted against paper money that stormy year of 1786, but the basic financial problem remained. Farms and homes were lost because the owners did not have the dollars to pay what they owed. Feeling rose against lawyers and judges who seemed to be growing rich by foreclosing mortgages. The hard-pressed farm-

Angry farmers under Daniel Shays marched on the court house at Springfield.

ers asked for laws by which they could pay off their debts with personal property—tools, clothes, furniture, real estate—but the legislature ended its meeting in July without providing any form of relief.

Rebellion shook Massachusetts. Mobs prevented the lower courts from meeting at Northampton and Worcester. An armed band seized the court house at Concord and drove the judge out of town. Some 800 rioters went even further at Great Barrington. They opened the jail and freed the prisoners.

In September another force, under tough old Daniel Shays, a veteran of the Revolu-tion, marched on Springfield, where the state supreme court was going to hear cases against debtors. The militia was called out, but Shays kept Springfield in such an up-roar that the court could not carry on its business. The militia, firing a cannon into Shays' ragtag army, killed three rebels.

Not until the following February did the militia finally end Shays' Rebellion. It had taken 4,000 men and thousands of dollars to restore law and order in Massa-chusetts. At the next election the people voted the governor out of office. In his place they put John Hancock, well known as a friend of liberty.

Massachusetts had to call out the militia before Shays' Rebellion could be ended.

"IN ORDER TO FORM A MORE PERFECT UNION"

Delegates of the new nation meet and draw up a constitution.

The Articles of Confederation, the agreements under which the United States operated, had not made the states into a true Union. There was almost no money with which to pay the national debt. Foreign affairs were loosely and poorly handled, and Indian warfare threatened the frontier. Connecticut and Pennsylvania were having a serious argument over who had the rights to the rich Wyoming Valley of Pennsylvania. New Jersey refused to pay her share of Confederation expenses because Congress could not settle her quarrels with New York and Pennsylvania.

Virginia's statesmen, including George Washington, James Madison, and Governor Edmund Randolph, took the lead in calling a convention to see what could be done. In May of 1787, delegates from eleven states met at Philadelphia in the room where the Declaration of Independence had been signed. New Hampshire was tardy in sending delegates and Rhode Island, always suspicious of her larger neighbors, was never represented.

Many of the delegates wanted to "patch up" the Articles of Confederation and make them more workable. But as the debates went on, the Articles were discarded. To take their place, a new plan of government was created—the Constitution. The British statesman William E. Gladstone would one

In 1787, delegates of the states met in Independence Hall in Philadelphia to draw up a plan for the government of the new nation. The result was the United States Constitution.

James Madison

day call it "the most wonderful work ever struck off at a given time by the brain and purpose of men."

Only twelve of the delegates to the Constitutional convention were past the age of fifty-four. Six were under thirty-one. Many remarkable men took part in the meetings. Among them were George Washington, Benjamin Franklin, and James Madison. Massachusetts sent Rufus King with his "strong expressive eye" and "sweet high-toned voice," and Elbridge Gerry, who "cherishes as his first virtue a love for his country." From Connecticut came Oliver Ellsworth, a judge of the Supreme Court, and Roger Sherman.

From South Carolina came John Rutledge, famous for his oratory, and Charles Pinckney, only twenty-four years of age. New York included among its delegates the gifted and sharp-tongued Alexander Hamilton. Pennsylvania sent Gouverneur Morris, who would have much to do with writing the final draft of the Constitution, and the learned James Wilson. Virginia's delegation included George Mason, a planter

who had written most of his state's constitution.

Yet there were some noted men who were absent. Thomas Jefferson and John Adams were abroad on diplomatic missions, Virginia's Patrick Henry and New York's George Clinton were at home. They were distrustful of the gathering and where it might lead the country.

George Washington was elected president of the convention, and Edmund Randolph presented to the delegates the "Virginia Plan." It called for a strong national government with three branches—Executive, Legislative, and Judicial. The Legislative branch would be divided into the Senate and the House of Representatives. The plan also called for representation in the legislative branch of government on the basis of population. The smaller states rebelled. They wanted equal representation, which was opposed by "the big three"—Virginia, Pennsylvania, and Massachusetts.

A "New Jersey plan" was proposed,

Benjamin Franklin

George Washington

No branch was to be too strong or too weak. The executive branch, under the President, could act independently and had command of the armed forces. These powers were checked and balanced by Congress, which controlled the President's appointments and had the power to start all actions concerning taxes and money.

Congress would write the nation's laws, but the President could veto any law he did not approve. Congress could then override the veto by a two-thirds vote. The Supreme Court could uphold the law or declare it unconstitutional.

The President and Vice-President were to be chosen for terms of four years, not by the direct vote of the people but by "electors." Each state was to select as many electors as it had representatives and senators. Meeting in their state capitals, these electors would vote for two men. The candidate receiving the highest number of votes would become President, and the candidate receiving the next highest Vice-President. Each state was

which would simply patch up the Articles of Confederation. This plan gave Congress some additional powers, including that of taxation, but prevented it from vetoing state laws. An executive committee, rather than a president, would be the head of the government.

The convention defeated the New Jersey plan. The delegates from the smaller states might have packed up and gone home, but they decided not to take the responsibility for breaking up the convention.

As the hot summer days rolled by, the delegates began to act in the spirit of compromise. Point by point they fought out their differences, carefully working out solutions to the most difficult kind of problems. In the end they created one of the great documents of history. It set up a practical system of government, flexible enough to be adapted to changing conditions. At the same time, it would not sacrifice the democratic principles of liberty and justice on which the nation was based.

With great wisdom, the delegates balanced the various powers of government.

Alexander Hamilton

287

Next page: *Debating the Constitution.*

given equal representation in the Senate, which was an advantage for the small states. Representation in the House of Representatives was according to population, which was an advantage for large states.

The Constitution was designed to be the law of the land and no state could pass laws conflicting with it. At the same time, many responsibilities were left to the states.

Not all the delegates were satisfied by the work of the convention. They had had to compromise on too many things. Yet they knew that without compromise there could be no democracy. Eighty-one-year-old Benjamin Franklin, whose body was feeble but whose mind was still sharp, pleaded for agreement among the delegates. His voice was too weak to be heard and James Wilson read his statement for him:

"I doubt . . . whether any other convention we can obtain may be able to make a better Constitution. . . . It therefore astonishes me, sir, to find this system approaching so near to perfection as it does. . . . Thus I consent, sir, to this Constitution, because I expect no better and because I am not sure that it is not the best. . . . I hope, therefore, that for our own sakes . . . and for the sake of posterity, we shall act heartily and unanimously in recommending this Constitution. . . . I cannot help expressing a wish that every member of the convention . . . would with me, on this occasion, doubt a little of his own infallibility, and . . . put his name to this instrument."

Of the forty-two delegates present at the time, thirty-nine signed. Then the document was made public—the document which begins with these noble words:

"We the People of the United States, in order to form a more perfect Union, establish Justice, insure domestic Tranquility, provide for the common Defence, promote the General Welfare, and secure the blessings of Liberty to Ourselves and our Posterity, do ordain and establish this Constitution for the United States of America. . . ."

LAUNCHING THE NEW GOVERNMENT

The Constitution is approved by the states and Washington is elected President.

Although the Constitutional Convention was over, there was still a struggle ahead. Before the Constitution was made legal, it had to be approved by at least nine states. Some people voted against the Constitution simply because it was new and different. Others feared that a strong central government would destroy the freedom of the states. And still others opposed the Constitution because it included no "Bill of Rights." They said it contained many safeguards of property rights, but no guarantees for the liberty of individuals. And so two groups sprang up—the Federalists, who favored the new Constitution, and the Anti-Federalists, who were against it.

Washington did much to win support for the Constitution. James Madison, Alexander Hamilton, and John Jay, who was soon to be the first Chief Justice of the Supreme Court, also supported it. They gave their views in a series of brilliant essays known as *The Federalist Papers*. And, perhaps the most important action of all, defenders of the Constitution won support for it by promising to work for a Bill of Rights as soon as the Constitution was approved by the states.

Delaware, Connecticut, Georgia, New Jersey, South Carolina, Pennsylvania, and Maryland were won over with the least trouble. In Massachusetts, where the farmers believed that the Constitution might favor business, the struggle was especially hard. It was not much better in New Hampshire, but finally, on June 21, 1788, this

On April 30, 1789, in New York City, George Washington took the oath of office and became the nation's first President.

little state became the ninth to ratify the Constitution, making it the supreme law of the land.

Virginia ratified the Constitution four days later, New York the following month. North Carolina would not agree until 1789, and then only after it was assured that a Bill of Rights would be added. Rhode Island finally signed on May 20, 1790.

Now that the nation had a constitution, it was time to set up the actual government. State legislatures named congressmen and electors to choose a President. Meeting in New York City on April 6, 1789, they made George Washington their unanimous choice for President. John Adams was named Vice-President. Formally notified of his election, Washington borrowed money from friends and started on the long journey from Mount Vernon to New York City.

Everywhere Washington stopped, crowds turned out to cheer him. On April 30, 1789, a barge carried him across New York Bay for his inauguration. On the deck of a sailboat, a chorus of ladies and gentlemen sang songs. From the Battery, cannon boomed a thirteen-gun salute. The streets were jammed to overflowing. Bands blared. Ladies stood at the windows of houses, waving handkerchiefs. Veterans of the Revolution cried out: "God bless you, General!"

Finally Washington stood on the balcony of the Federal Building. To encourage the nation's young textile industry, he wore a neat brown suit that had been made in America. He felt ill and faint. But he said: "I do solemnly swear that I will faithfully execute the Office of the President of the United States, and will to the best of my ability preserve, protect and defend the Constitution of the United States."

WASHINGTON AS PRESIDENT

The new government deals with money matters and foreign affairs and adopts the Bill of Rights.

When Washington became President of the United States he faced many problems, and one of the most important was that the country needed money. He chose Alexander Hamilton, his aide-de-camp during the Revolution, as his Secretary of the Treasury. The warm friendship between the two men aroused jealousy in other members of the government, and in time caused serious trouble. Nevertheless, Hamilton was a wise choice, for he was truly a genius of finance.

Hamilton went about his difficult tasks with great boldness of imagination. Both the national government and the individual states had borrowed money to carry on the War for Independence. Now Hamilton proposed not only that the national government pay its debts in full to European creditors, but also that it pay the debts of the states. He pushed through his plan by skillful political maneuvering. He won the support of the Southerners by agreeing that the new national capital city should be located in the South, on the banks of the Potomac River.

Whatever Hamilton did, he fought hard and he fought to win. When the tariff of 1790 failed to raise the money he needed, he suggested a tax on whiskey. Congressmen from the South and the West raised a howl. People in their districts used whiskey to trade for manufactured goods, iron, and salt. They said the tax hurt the poor. Besides, it was too much like the English

Jefferson and Hamilton disagreed on how the country should be run.

system that allowed agents of the king to snoop into local affairs. Again Hamilton stood his ground, again he won.

Hamilton was no sooner out of one fight than he was in another. When he took office as secretary, there were only three banks in America: in Philadelphia, New York, and Boston. To give the country a sounder banking system, Hamilton proposed the establishment of a Bank of the United States with branches in various cities. It could issue reliable money, collect taxes, and in other ways make it easier for Americans to conduct business.

Opponents called the plan for a government-run bank unconstitutional, and among them was Thomas Jefferson, who was now Secretary of State. For once Washington hesitated in his support of Hamilton. Then Hamilton sent him a brilliantly written memorandum justifying the founding of the bank, and the President signed the bill authorizing it.

So Hamilton had won again—but Jefferson's distrust of him grew. The two men were opposites in almost every way. Jefferson was awkward in debate, while Hamilton was quick of speech. Jefferson believed firmly in democracy, while Hamilton referred to the common people as "that great beast." Each was suspicious of the other, and meetings between the two were uncomfortable. Yet both were great men, and Washington needed them both.

The President could have little complaint about the way Jefferson handled the extremely difficult foreign relations of the young nation. Both Britain and Spain dreamed of conquest and expansion beyond the Appalachians, both plotted with the Indians. The British still held illegal fur posts at places like Detroit and Mackinac. The Spanish occupied Natchez on the Mississippi and were pushing farther north. They hoped to stir up so much feeling in Kentucky and Tennessee that these two states, which had only recently become part of the nation, would withdraw from the Union. The British and the Spanish were playing a hardheaded, cold-blooded game. The United States was too weak to protect its borders. What could she do but stand by as rich lands were nibbled away?

But Jefferson took advantage of the rivalries among the European nations. He played the British against the Spanish in a dispute over fur posts on the Pacific coast. The result was that England, who had refused to send a diplomatic envoy to the United States, now changed her mind. When France went to war against Prussia and Austria, Jefferson held Britain and Spain in line by withholding aid from France. In the end, Britain agreed to leave the northwestern fur posts. Spain wanted to make peace with France. Knowing that Britain would not like this, she decided to strengthen her friendship with the United States, to whom she gave free use of the Mississippi and trading privileges at New Orleans.

THE BILL OF RIGHTS

While the United States was making a place for itself among the nations of the world, there was an important development at home. In 1789 the first Congress passed ten amendments to the Constitution, known as "the Bill of Rights." Submitted by James Madison in the House of Representatives, they provided basic guarantees of individual liberties for all the nation's citizens.

The first amendment guaranteed freedom of religion, freedom of the press, and the right peaceably to assemble and to petition the government for "a redress of grievances" (the remedying or correcting of unfair situations).

The next three amendments guaranteed a militia and the right to bear arms, forbade lodging troops in people's homes in time of peace, and declared a citizen's home secure against invasion and search except by permission of a judge—liberties dearly prized by those who remembered the struggles of the Revolution.

Amendments five through eight guaranteed trial by jury, protected citizens against unreasonable arrest or cruel punishment, and provided that no person should be "deprived of life, liberty or property without due process of law."

The final two amendments defined the division of powers between federal and state governments.

By 1791, the amendments were ratified by the states and became part of the Constitution.

VICTORY AT FALLEN TIMBERS

"Mad Anthony" Wayne is sent to put down an Indian uprising.

It was remarkable, really, how much was being accomplished in these first few years. By trial and error, the young nation was moving ahead—in finance, in foreign affairs, in expanding its basic laws. And all the time the country was growing. Vermont became a state in 1791. Kentucky was admitted in 1792, Tennessee in 1796.

But there was serious trouble in the region north of the Ohio River. The Indians, stirred up by the British, were becoming

The United States in 1792, showing the Northwest Territory, scene of Indian uprisings.

dangerously restless. Washington had kept an old friend, General Arthur St. Clair, as governor of the Northwest Territory, but soon reports suggested that St. Clair might be napping on the job. Indians were massacring settlers. Traders were being killed or driven away.

A force of militia—about 1,500 ragged and poorly trained men—invaded the Indiana Territory in October of 1790. Five Indian towns and 20,000 bushels of corn were destroyed. The Indians counterattacked viciously. The militia retreated, and the settlements were open to a new wave of murder, fire, and robbery.

St. Clair now awakened from his nap. With a force of 2,000 men, assembled at Cincinnati, he set off against the Indians. The old general advanced at a snail's pace, stopping often to build forts. The army's food supply shrank to almost nothing; every day more men deserted. In November, 1791, St. Clair and his weary, quarrelsome army were encamped on a branch of the Wabash when the Indians struck. The shriek of their war whoops shook St. Clair from his tent. His defeat amounted to disaster, but for once he moved swiftly. In one day he retreated as far as he had advanced in ten.

All of the region north of the Ohio—and Kentucky as well—was now threatened with even worse terror. The Indians were led by Joseph Brant, who had a cunning mind and a ruthless heart. When the news of St. Clair's troubles reached Philadelphia, which was now the national capital, the President was furious. Washington loved the frontier and wanted it protected. He turned to "Mad Anthony" Wayne to restore peace to the Ohio country.

Wayne was an efficient officer. First he drilled his men in the fundamentals of fighting. Then in the winter of 1793-94, he moved to Fort Greenville, seventy-five miles north of Cincinnati. With warm weather, Wayne began his advance into the Indian country. He passed one deserted village after another, until he reached a region where a tornado had uprooted the trees.

In this "land of fallen timbers," Wayne met the Indians. There were Miamis, Shawnees, Ottawas, Chippewas, Potawatomis, Sauk and Fox, and a small band of Iroquois. The Americans charged with fixed bayonets. Cavalrymen spurred their horses over the tree stumps. In less than an hour the Battle of Fallen Timbers ended in a complete rout of the Indians. A year later they signed a treaty that gave most of Ohio to the United States.

295

THE POLITICAL POT BEGINS TO BOIL

*The Jefferson-Hamilton feud
leads to the formation of
America's first political parties.*

With peace secure the young nation began stretching its muscles, making progress in many ways. In 1788, *Nicholas Pike's Arithmetic* was first published at Newburyport, Massachusetts. George Washington was among those who endorsed the book, and it became widely used in schoolrooms throughout the country. That same year Noah Webster's *The American Spelling Book* appeared; in time it would sell 70,000,000 copies. In 1792, at Sterling, Massachusetts, Robert Baily Thomas began publishing *The Farmer's Almanac,* which would have a longer life than any other American periodical.

The previous year, George Washington had accepted the services of Pierre Charles L'Enfant, a young French engineer who had served with Lafayette during the Revolution. L'Enfant was to plan a new city on the Potomac, a city which was to be the nation's capital.

It was in this period that two men produced inventions that would change American life and history. One was Samuel Slater. At Pawtucket, Rhode Island, in 1790, he constructed America's first successful power-driven cotton-spinning machine. But cotton was not yet profitable because of the high cost of separating the seed from the fiber. The work was done by hand, and a slave could clean little more than a pound of cotton a day.

Not long after Slater had set up his machine, a young Yankee left New England to take a teaching job in Georgia. His name was Eli Whitney, and when he reached the

South he found that his job had disappeared. Although he had never seen cotton or cottonseed before, he turned his mind to the problem of cleaning the fiber. In 1793 he invented the cotton gin, which could clean more cotton in a single day than a slave could in a month. Soon cotton became "white gold" to the South, and plantations began to prosper. Large numbers of field hands were needed to raise the crop, and the South built its future on an increased use of Negro slaves.

Even though America was moving ahead, Washington found his years as President

*Eli Whitney's cotton gin was a simple device for cleaning cotton
fiber. It worked so well that cotton became the South's biggest crop.*

growing more and more unhappy. The feud
between Alexander Hamilton and Thomas
Jefferson steadily worsened. Each had different views of government, each had his
supporters, and this led to the formation
of the new nation's first political parties.

Hamilton believed in a strong, central-
ized government and in encouraging business and industry. In foreign affairs, he
favored the British. His views attracted
wealthy merchants, big landowners in the
North, and small businessmen. These were
the Federalists.

The opposition—the Anti-Federalists—
was made up of Southern landowners, of
craftsmen, workers, and small farmers. They
were against Hamilton's programs of taxation and were pro-French. They sympa-
thized with France's struggle against tyranny, which to them seemed much like
their own revolution. They found their
leader in Jefferson.

First calling themselves the Federal Republicans and later the Democratic-Republicans, they made no effort to oppose Washington for the presidency in 1792. But
John Adams, a Federalist running for re-
election as Vice-President, was opposed by

297

President John Adams

into a nasty little civil war. The mails were robbed so that reports on the rebels could not reach Philadelphia. Washington acted vigorously, calling out 15,000 militiamen. In November, 1794, they reached the scene of trouble, but they found no rebel army to fight. A number of suspects were arrested, and two were tried and found guilty. Washington believed he had upheld the spirit of the law, so he immediately pardoned these offenders. The Whiskey Rebellion was over.

JOHN ADAMS SUCCEEDS WASHINGTON

Adams suffers from the political battles around him and is bitter when he leaves office.

Thomas Jefferson's eye was firmly fixed on the presidential election in 1796, and his followers continued to attack the Federalists as the party of "tyrants, taxes and Tories." Meanwhile, the Federalists were having trouble within their own ranks. There was bad feeling between two of their leaders—John Adams and Alexander Hamilton. Adams was more moderate in his views than Hamilton.

Hamilton was not popular enough to be elected President himself, so he tried to block Adams' election. With the aid of Southern Federalists in Congress, he schemed to divide the electoral college vote evenly between Adams and Thomas Pinckney of South Carolina. Then it would be up to Congress to decide who should become President. But John Adams outmaneuvered Hamilton. Supported by eighteen New Englanders, he won the presidency, while Hamilton's old foe, Jefferson, became Vice-President. The two highest offices in the land were held by men of opposing parties.

George Clinton of New York. Although Adams won, he failed to carry five states— Virginia, New York, North Carolina, Georgia and Kentucky—and the Federalists lost control in Congress.

Jefferson's revolt was just beginning. The formation of "Democratic Societies" during the summer of 1793 kept the political pot boiling. All sorts of charges were made against Washington. The Father of the Country was no longer a man who could do no wrong.

Hamilton's excise tax on whiskey outraged many people. In western Pennsylvania, tax collectors were driven off. The men who did this were ordered to cross the Alleghenies and stand trial in Philadelphia. An angry mob awaited the marshal who came to make the arrests. The home of the inspector of excise was destroyed and some of the soldiers guarding it were killed.

The Whiskey Rebellion now had flamed

During the late 1790's, the British and the French menaced American ships at sea.

By this time, Britain and France were at war. Both countries disliked the fact that America was neutral and insisted on the right to seize American ships on the high seas. French diplomats offered to stop these acts of piracy if they were given bribes for themselves and a loan of $12,500,000 for their country.

Adams refused. He substituted the letters X, Y, Z for the names of the diplomats and published their letters. The nation was outraged, and rallied to the cry: "Millions for defense, but not one cent for tribute!" Washington agreed to take command of the army in case of a war with France. Shipyards turned out a few frigates, marking the beginning of the American navy. The U. S. frigate *Constellation* captured one

French frigate and defeated another in a furious battle fought on a stormy sea.

At home, Adams started a different kind of war when he signed the Alien and Sedition Acts. These were set up by the Federalists to make difficulties for people sympathetic to the French—people who were flocking to Jefferson's party. Under the Acts, the President could banish from the country any alien (any person not a citizen) he considered dangerous. Anyone who wrote "scandalous or malicious" articles about the President or Congress could be jailed. More than that, the time a person had to wait before becoming a naturalized citizen was lengthened from five to fourteen years.

Clearly these acts did away with freedom

The U. S. frigate Constellation *fought well in the undeclared naval war with France.*

which was now the nation's capital. He complained that the executive mansion was cold, drafty, and uncomfortable. His wife, Abigail, hung her wash in the unfinished East Room. The only interruption in the quarreling that surrounded him came at the death of George Washington on December 14, 1799. Everywhere people mourned this great American who was "first in war, first in peace, first in the hearts of his countrymen."

The interruption was brief, and Adams' political war went on. Hamilton still believed himself the rightful head of the Federalists. He made no secret that he was plotting to rid the party of Adams as its presidential candidate. Adams hit back hard. He dismissed Hamilton's supporters from his cabinet and finally won the nomination. Charles Cotesworth Pinckney, a Revolutionary general and a South Carolina delegate to the Constitutional Convention, was his vice-presidential candidate. The Democratic-Republicans nominated Jefferson for President, with Aaron Burr of New York as his running-mate. Burr had served in the army and in the Senate.

The country would not soon forget the election of 1800. Hamilton attacked Adams without mercy, and Jefferson called him an enemy of liberty. Federalist clergymen rallied to Adams, calling Jefferson an infidel who would pull down the churches if elected. The campaign divided the nation; New England was for Adams, the South for Jefferson. There was even talk that if Jefferson won, New England might be forced to secede from the Union.

The electors met in December. As expected, New England solidly supported Adams. New Jersey and Delaware also supported him, and he drew a scattering of

of speech and the press. A congressman from Vermont was jailed and a number of Republican editors brought to trial. Jefferson and Madison led the opposition against this "Federalist tyranny." In a series of resolutions they argued for "states rights," declaring that whenever the national government assumed a power not granted in the Constitution, "its acts are unauthoritative, void and of no force." In time the Alien and Sedition Acts expired. Although Adams had opposed the Acts, and although he had done little to apply them, he suffered from the political explosion they created.

In the last months of his presidency Adams moved his family into the recently completed White House in Washington,

301

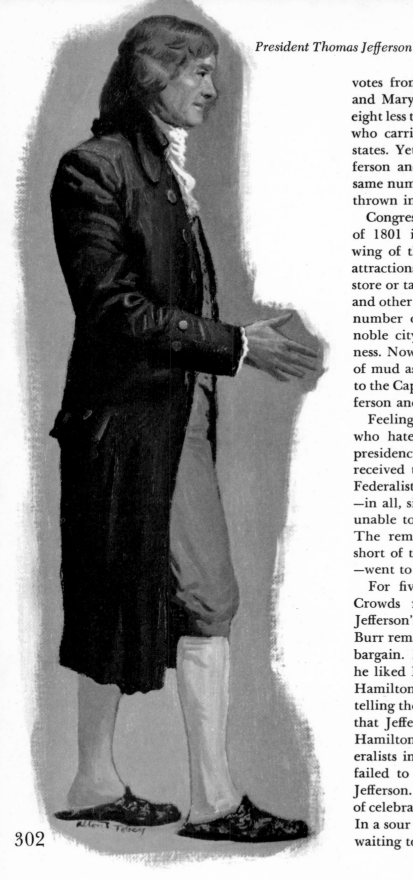

President Thomas Jefferson

votes from Pennsylvania, North Carolina, and Maryland. Adams' total was sixty-five, eight less than the Democratic-Republicans', who carried New York and the Southern states. Yet nothing had been decided. Jefferson and Burr had received exactly the same number of votes, and the election was thrown into the House of Representatives.

Congress began voting in mid-February of 1801 in the recently completed north wing of the Capitol. The city offered few attractions beyond a church, an occasional store or tavern, a clutter of boarding houses and other residences, some brick kilns and a number of huts. Eventually a grand and noble city would arise out of the wilderness. Now, however, the streets were rivers of mud as congressmen walked up the hill to the Capitol to make a choice between Jefferson and Burr.

Feelings ran high. Most of the Federalists, who hated Jefferson, wanted to give the presidency to Burr. On the first ballot he received the support of the New England Federalists, Delaware and South Carolina —in all, six states. Maryland and Vermont, unable to make a choice, split their votes. The remaining eight states—or one state short of the number necessary for election —went to Jefferson.

For five days the deadlock continued. Crowds roamed the streets, demanding Jefferson's election. In New York City, Burr remained silent, refusing to make any bargain. Hamilton disliked Jefferson, but he liked Burr even less. Behind the scenes Hamilton worked on his Federalist friends, telling them that Burr could not be trusted, that Jefferson must be the choice. Finally, Hamilton swung the election when the Federalists in divided Maryland and Vermont failed to appear and these states went to Jefferson. News of his victory set off a wave of celebrations. People danced in the streets. In a sour mood Adams left the city without waiting to see his successor inaugurated.

A PRESIDENT IN CARPET SLIPPERS

Buying Louisiana from Napoleon, Jefferson doubles the size of the nation.

The British Ambassador

Throughout his life Thomas Jefferson had always thought and acted in his own way, and he did not change when he became President. The tall, red-headed Virginian shocked the British ambassador, who appeared at the White House in a splendid uniform and dress sword, by greeting him in a pair of old carpet slippers. Jefferson did not care. He liked the freedom of slouching around in carpet slippers.

As President, Jefferson was willing to make compromises. "Every difference of opinion is not difference of principle," he said in his inaugural address. "We are all Republicans—we are all Federalists." His policies were much like those Adams would have followed if he had been re-elected. By cutting government spending, Jefferson reduced the national debt and lowered taxes. He ended the excise tax on whiskey. He encouraged the expansion of northwestern territory, and in 1803 Ohio became a state.

In Europe, Napoleon Bonaparte was now the ruler of France, and he was planning to build an empire in the New World. He hoped to make Haiti, an island in the Caribbean Sea, a center for growing sugar and other tropical products. He would bring in food for his sugar growers from Louisiana —and the fact that the Louisiana Territory belonged to Spain did not bother him a bit.

Napoleon secretly arranged a deal with Spain. In return for Louisiana, he offered to give to the son-in-law of the King of Spain a principality in Italy, which was then also under French rule. When Jefferson learned of the deal, he was greatly worried. He

303

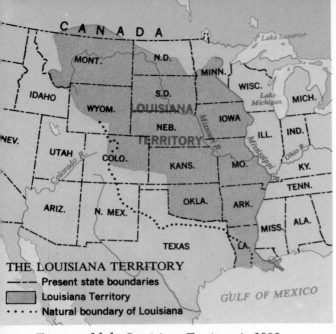

THE LOUISIANA TERRITORY
- - - Present state boundaries
▨ Louisiana Territory
• • • Natural boundary of Louisiana

France sold the Louisiana Territory in 1803.

feared having the French on the borders of the United States. He also feared that the Mississippi would be closed to American trade, and, in fact, in 1802, Americans did lose some of their trading rights in New Orleans. Something had to be done, and in 1803 Jefferson sent James Monroe to France with instructions to purchase New Orleans.

Before Monroe arrived, the American envoy in France received unexpected news. Napoleon was ready to sell not only New Orleans, but all of Louisiana. A revolution and an outbreak of yellow fever in Haiti had ended Napoleon's interest in that island. Besides, he was now plotting a war against England and needed money. He of-

Alexander Hamilton fired into the air in his duel with Aaron Burr.

fered the United States a "noble bargain": about 828,000 square miles of land, between the Mississippi and the Rocky Mountains, for $15,000,000.

Jefferson was astonished. But he had a problem—the Constitution gave him no power to make such a purchase. Not too long ago, he himself had attacked the Federalists for taking powers not granted by the Constitution. Yet how could he pass by this opportunity to double the size of the nation? And he had to act quickly, for Napoleon was the kind of man who might very well change his mind. The President decided that the opportunity was more important than the principle and authorized

the Louisiana Purchase. The Senate approved it by a vote of twenty-six to five and the House by a vote of ninety to twenty-five.

A political storm arose. The Federalists' strength was mainly in New England. They were afraid that any new states formed of the Louisiana Territory would support the ideas and policies of Jefferson. Again they said that soon New England would be forced to leave the Union. The states of New York and New Jersey would join New England and set up a northern confederacy with its own government.

The Federalists knew that this scheme could not succeed without New York, and for help they turned to Aaron Burr. The

But Burr fired at his political foe, and Hamilton died of his wound.

Jeffersonians had never forgiven Burr for trying to defeat Jefferson for the presidency in 1801. Burr was quite willing to listen to the Federalists if they would help him become governor of New York.

Once more Alexander Hamilton threw all his political power against Burr, and as a result Burr lost the election. The defeat clearly told the Federalists that their dreams had died. They had failed to win New York, and without it there could be no confederacy. Moreover, the Federalists now had no chance of stopping Jefferson's re-election.

Burr, the man without a party, soon became a man without a country. Furious with Hamilton, Burr challenged his old foe to a duel. Hamilton accepted, and the two met on a misty July morning in 1804 on the banks of the Hudson at Weehawken, New Jersey. Hamilton fired into the air. Burr took careful aim, and Hamilton was mortally wounded.

Guilty of murder, Burr escaped into the Southwest. No one can say for certain what wild schemes filled his mind. He plotted with all kinds of persons, including British and Spanish ministers, and perhaps he did plan to set up his own independent state in Louisiana. Captured as he was sailing a force down the Mississippi, he was brought to trial for treason in 1807. He was acquitted for lack of evidence, but he was in disgrace and fled to Europe.

EXPLORING THE CONTINENT

Lewis and Clark head an expedition to explore the Northwest.

Even before the Louisiana Purchase, Jefferson had wanted to send an expedition to explore the vast wilderness of the West. One of the reasons was the disturbing news of

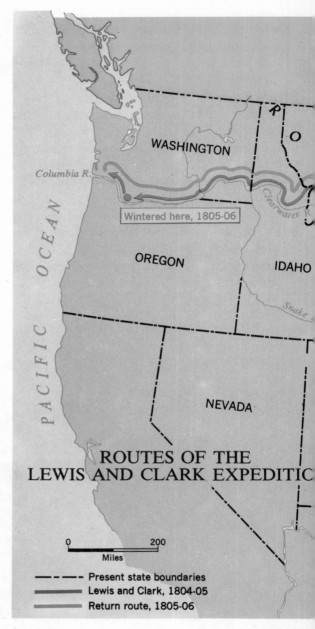

ROUTES OF THE LEWIS AND CLARK EXPEDITIO[N]

0   200
Miles

----- Present state boundaries
——— Lewis and Clark, 1804-05
——— Return route, 1805-06

the British in the region west of the Mississippi. American fur traders in St. Louis were complaining of competition from such British-owned organizations as the Hudson's Bay Company and the Northwest Company, which had been operating in this region since 1783. A third company—the Mackinaw Company—also was pushing into the territory that one day would become Minnesota and Wisconsin.

Jefferson wanted to know the facts, and

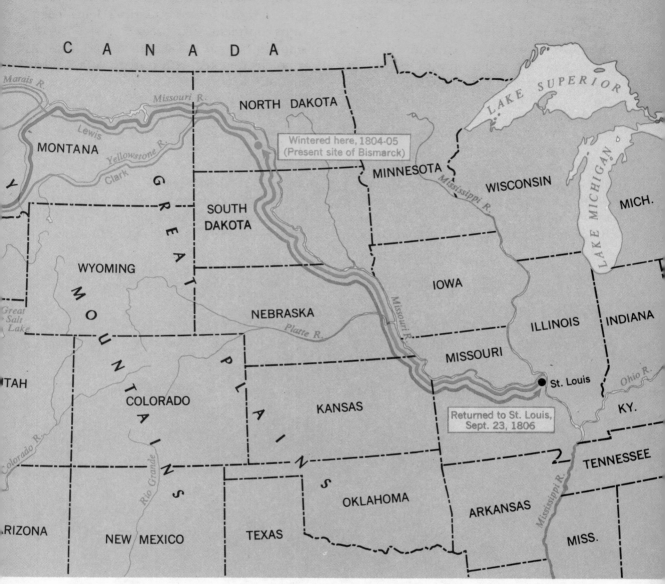

Wintered here, 1804-05
(Present site of Bismarck)

Returned to St. Louis,
Sept. 23, 1806

he wanted a survey of the new territory purchased from France. He authorized an expedition under his private secretary, Meriwether Lewis, and William Clark (brother of the famous George Rogers Clark). They were to explore the Missouri River, discover the source of the Mississippi River, and find a river leading to the Pacific.

In the summer of 1804, these explorers and their party traveled 1,600 miles into the country of the Mandan Indians. They camped for the winter at the mouth of the Missouri (near the site of present-day Bismarck, North Dakota). Scouts brought back a variety of gifts for Jefferson: the horns of a mountain ram, skins of the red fox, white hare, marten, and yellow bear, articles of Indian dress, a box of plants, "and three cases containing a burrowing squirrel, a prairie hen, and four magpies, all alive."

With spring, Lewis and Clark pushed up the Missouri into Montana. Guided by 307

Sacagawea, the wife of a French guide and the sister of an important Indian chief, they crossed the Rocky Mountains. They talked with Indians of many tribes, who treated the travelers with great friendliness. Their journals became crammed with information about the geography, plant life, and animals in the unknown interior of America. They discovered the source of the Bitter Root River, branched off into other streams, and so came at last to the great Columbia River, which carried them in November of 1805 to their first sight of the Pacific.

On the return journey the party divided. Lewis followed the sources of the Marias River, and Clark the Yellowstone River.

Other explorers, under Lieutenant Zebulon M. Pike, striking out from St. Louis, also were adding to America's knowledge of its continent. Pike pressed up the Mississippi to beyond the mouth of the Minnesota River, talked with Indians, established the authority of the United States government, and selected the site for Fort Snelling. The following year, 1806, he pushed westward and gave his name to snowy Pikes Peak in the Rocky Mountains.

These expeditions showed that the continent was rich in opportunities for new settlements and trade. In time, thirteen states would be formed from America's great bargain—the Louisiana Purchase.

In 1807, the British seized four sailors from the U. S. frigate Chesapeake.

VICTORY IN THE MEDITERRANEAN

American ships put down the pirates of North Africa, but are no match for the British navy.

For years the Barbary states, along the north shore of Africa, had grown rich by demanding the payment of tribute from all vessels entering the Mediterranean Sea. The United States had followed the example of older nations by making payments to these pirate states. But the greedy Pasha of Tripoli grew dissatisfied with this arrangement early in Jefferson's years as President. The United States had a weak navy. If American vessels wished to sail the Mediterranean, they must pay more.

At the Pasha's orders, the United States flag was cut down on the consulate in a declaration of war. Pirate craft from Tripoli boarded American ships, seized cargoes, and imprisoned crews and passengers. For two years such robbery and insult in the Mediterranean simply proved the Pasha right. The American navy was unable to protect its citizens on the high seas.

The bitterest blow came in 1803 when

Outraged, Congress passed an act that stopped trade with Britain and France.

the *Philadelphia* ran aground during a battle. Captain and crew were jailed and the ship was seized as a prize. But on a February night in 1804, a small force under Captain Stephen Decatur entered the harbor of Tripoli. Under the guns of the Pasha's castle, it boarded and burned the *Philadelphia*.

Congress now decided to raise the money to send a squadron capable of handling the Barbary pirates. The harbor of Tripoli was blockaded and the Pasha's vessels constantly attacked. The pirates soon granted freedom to American ships in the Mediterranean.

But the nation's troubles on the high seas were not yet over. By 1806, war between France and England caught American shipping in a squeeze. Britain blockaded the European coast from the French port of Brest to the Elbe River, and France blockaded the British Isles. Each nation seized any American ship suspected of trading with its enemy.

Jefferson knew the United States was not prepared for a war. The British knew it, too, and refused to negotiate any kind of settlement. Arguing that many seamen had deserted the Royal Navy to sign up for higher wages on American ships, Britain declared that she had the right to stop and search American ships and take off sailors suspected of deserting.

On June 22, 1807, off Hampton Roads, the British man-of-war *Leopard* fired upon the American frigate *Chesapeake*. Three American sailors as well as one British deserter were removed.

"British Outrage!" screamed the American newspapers, and Congress had to take action. It passed an embargo act that prohibited any vessel from leaving an American port for a foreign country, and a nonimportation act that said no goods from England and France could be brought into an American port.

These policies, which were supported by Jefferson, crippled the nation's trade. Ships

310

General William Henry Harrison

Tecumseh

stood idle at the wharves. Sailors roamed the streets, unable to find work. Although there was a great deal of smuggling in Maine and Georgia, trade fell from $108,000,000 in 1807 to $22,000,000 in 1808. The embargoes were no solution to the basic problem of British-American relations. That would not be solved until a war was fought.

THE MANY FACES OF TROUBLE

Madison becomes President
and has difficulties
both at home and abroad.

Nearing the end of his second term as President, Jefferson faced revolt even within the ranks of his own party. The rebellious Democratic-Republicans were called the "Quids." They were led by John Randolph of Virginia, once one of the President's closest friends. They fought Jefferson's legislative program in Congress. They also hoped to make James Monroe the next President, although Jefferson had already chosen James Madison as his successor.

Meanwhile, the New England Federalists played their old game of threatening secession and even received into their inner circles a British agent from Canada. But many states still relied on their legislatures rather than on a popular vote to select electors for President. Jefferson, as his party's leader, was able to control the legislators and beat off all the opposition. Madison easily won the election of 1808.

James Madison was almost as brilliant as Jefferson, and just as stubborn. A sickly child who received his early education from private tutors, he managed to graduate from the College of New Jersey (now Princeton) at the age of twenty.

Madison was told that he could not hope 311

Stirred up by the British, Tecumseh led the Indians in raid after raid.

to succeed in Virginia politics without giving the voters a free drink of whiskey on election day. He replied that then he would rather lose—and he did. Appointed to the governor's council, he fought for religious freedom in Virginia. As a delegate to the Constitutional Convention of 1787, he contributed many ideas, and he became known as the "Father of the Constitution." He was Jefferson's chief lieutenant in the political war between the Democratic-Republicans and Hamilton's Federalists, and then was Jefferson's Secretary of State. When he came to the White House, he had a thorough knowledge of the nation's problems.

At home Madison's troubles wore many faces. In Congress his enemies defeated an effort to renew the charter of the Bank of the United States. If war should come, the government would lack the money and credit it would need. A group of congressmen wanted to take over Florida, which was still owned by Spain, an ally of England. In the Northwest the Indians once more were being stirred to revolt by British agents, and the powerful Shawnee chief Tecumseh could aid these British schemes.

The governor of the Indiana Territory was William Henry Harrison, who had learned how to fight during the Revolution. Harrison summoned Tecumseh to the Ohio state capital at Vincennes, to make peace. The conference began badly on an August day in 1810, when Harrison asked the chief to sit near his "father," meaning himself.

Stiffly, Tecumseh replied: "The sun is my father, and the earth is my mother, and on her bosom I will repose."

He was finally beaten at the Tippecanoe River by William Henry Harrison.

Tecumseh offered no hope for peace unless the white men returned all the lands they held along the Wabash and White Rivers. Indian raids the following year ended Harrison's patience. With some 1,100 volunteers, he marched on an Indian village on the Tippecanoe River.

Near here, on a raw day in November of 1811, the Indians asked for a parley. Harrison agreed, but he expected trickery. "Boys," he said to his men while they waited, "if they strike, keep your aim low."

Before dawn, the Indians attacked. Harrison waited for daylight, when he could use his cavalry. "Now ride them down," he ordered. Harrison's cavalrymen fought like frontiersmen, with sabers, clubs, and hunting knives. Tecumseh fled. Next day, in the Indian village, Harrison discovered some guns that had been made in England.

In April of 1812 there was a series of Indian raids from Fort Dearborn (later Chicago) to the Ohio River. Younger men from the frontier had now taken seats in Congress. They became the "War Hawks" who cried that the time had come to settle with England. Massacre along the frontier, the impressment of American seamen, insults to American statesmen—the "War Hawks" built their case against the British point by point.

Finally, Madison asked for a declaration of war against England, and on June 18, 1812, Congress agreed. At that moment in England, the royal government was taking steps to stop many of the acts that had aroused America, but this information reached Washington too late.

313

THE WAR OF 1812

*Again, British troops march
on American soil and British
and American ships meet in battle.*

"Mr. Madison's War"—that was what Madison's political foes called the War of 1812. The nation was divided in its opinion of the war, as was shown in the election of that year. De Witt Clinton of New York, supported by a combination of Federalists and Democratic-Republicans, would have won if he had been able to get the electoral college vote of Pennsylvania.

Madison was re-elected, mainly because

of the support of the "War Hawks." They wanted action, and he planned a campaign to end the British threat along the frontier. The War Department worked out a three-pronged invasion of Canada from Detroit, Niagara, and Lake Champlain. The plan seemed a good one, and so it was—on paper. In practice, it fell apart.

A force of about 2,000 men under General William Hull, Governor of the Michigan Territory, moved from Detroit into Canada. Overconfident, Hull issued a proclamation inviting Canadians to join him in overthrowing their royal masters. The British only laughed. Seizing Fort Mackinac, they drove Hull back into Detroit. He was frightened by what the Indians might do if he held out, and quickly surrendered.

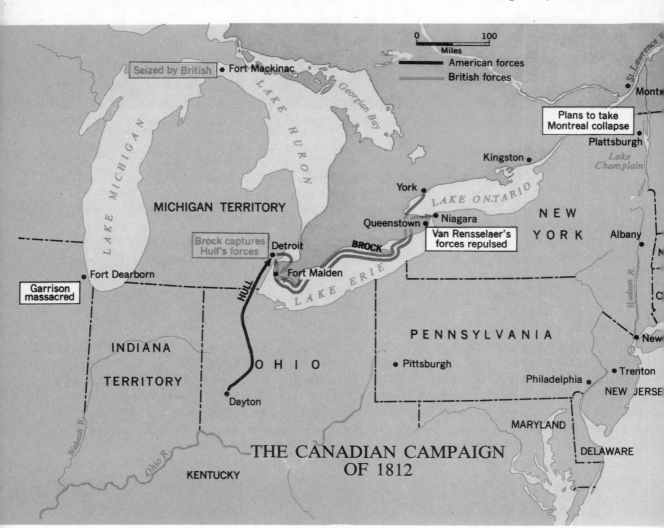

THE CANADIAN CAMPAIGN
OF 1812

The Constitution *defeated the British frigate* Guerrière *in a famous naval victory.*

With Detroit captured, the British swept easily to the foot of Lake Michigan and took Fort Dearborn.

British General Isaac Brock, who had bagged Hull, moved next to Niagara. General Stephen Van Rensselaer of New York crossed the Niagara River and attacked Brock at Queenston Heights, in Canada. Van Rensselaer had some 6,000 troops, about half of them regulars. The rest were militiamen from New York. Arguing that they were not required to fight beyond their own borders, they refused to support the regulars. In a disastrous retreat, the Americans were driven across the river. A third force, which was supposed to attack Montreal, did not even budge from its camps.

Meanwhile, the "War Hawks" wanted to annex Florida, which was owned by Spain. Congress recognized Spain as a "friendly" power and refused.

Anyone could see that on the land the war was going badly. But the war at sea was another story. In early August the *Constitution*—"Old Ironsides"—was roaming the Atlantic in search of British prey. She sighted the enemy frigate *Guerrière* and went after her. The *Guerrière* circled, fired two broadsides that fell short, then ran up topsails and jib to make a race to safety. The *Constitution* bore down steadily until she was "within half pistol-shot." Her guns blasted the *Guerrière*, knocking down her masts and tearing her sails into ribbons. The British vessel was scarcely worth towing into port.

315

Other naval victories that summer and fall filled Americans with pride. The *Essex* captured the British frigate *Alert* south of Chesapeake Bay. The *Wasp* bagged the *Frolic* in southern waters. The British frigate *Macedonian* was captured off the Madeiras, and in December the *Constitution* sank the *Java* off the coast of Brazil.

The winter of 1812-13 gave American forces a chance to prepare for another campaign against Canada. At the head of troops assembled in the Ohio Valley was William Henry Harrison, who had scattered Tecumseh's Indians at Tippecanoe. Harrison would soon face his old Indian foe again, for Tecumseh was now allied with the British. Although the Americans lost one battle, in two others they kept the British from capturing Forts Meigs and Stephenson. But Harrison realized that the Americans could never regain Detroit unless they controlled Lake Erie.

FIGHTING IN CANADA

Even at sea the war was now going badly. The British navy blockaded American ports from Savannah to New York. Thirty miles off Boston, the U.S. frigate *Chesapeake* met the British frigate *Shannon*. As the *Chesapeake*'s captain, James Lawrence, lay dying, he said, "Don't give up the ship!" But his vessel was no match for the *Shannon*. It was captured and brought into Halifax.

Then, in September, Captain Oliver Hazard Perry set sail on Lake Erie in search of the British navy. He found it on September 10, 1813, off Sandusky, Ohio.

The battle opened just before noon, and within two hours his flagship, the *Lawrence*, was disabled and her flag came down. Perry boarded the *Niagara*, turned away from the painful sight, and gave the signal for "close action." The *Niagara* went straight at the enemy, her guns blazing. Before the day closed, Perry wrote his famous letter to Harrison:

His flagship disabled, Perry transferred to another ship to win the Battle of Lake Erie.

British guns disabled the Lawrence.

Dear General,

We have met the enemy, and they are ours. Two ships, two brigs, one schooner, and one sloop. Yours with very great respect and esteem,

O. H. Perry

Harrison sent his troops marching northward. The British left Detroit, but Harrison pursued them thirty miles to the east until he reached the Thames River in Ontario, Canada. The battle was a furious affair. Harrison rode down the British regulars with the same sort of reckless, slashing cavalry charge that had won at Tippecanoe. The British surrendered.

On the left, protected by a swamp, Tecumseh stood his ground. When the Americans clashed with the Indians, "the terrible voice of Tecumseh could be distinctly heard, encouraging his warriors." The swamp fight turned into a wild tangle— men yelling, clubbing, shooting, slashing with knife and bayonet. The Indians clustered around the gallant Tecumseh. In an instant, it seemed, a hundred bullets hissed about him. Then Tecumseh pitched forward. The Indians fell back, and the Battle of the Thames had ended in a victory for Harrison.

In April, General Dearborn crossed Lake Ontario and captured York (now Toronto) and a month later held control of the Niagara River. But he was an inefficient officer —and by early winter the British not only held the New York side of the Niagara, but had also burned Lewiston and Buffalo. In the South, the month of August brought a frightful massacre by Creek warriors at Fort Mims on the Alabama River. Andrew Jackson rallied the militia in Tennessee and Georgia to deal with the Indians.

FROM LUNDY'S LANE TO NEW ORLEANS

Americans take the offensive, but their last victory is won after the peace has been signed.

After the war had continued for about two years, there were some important changes. Britain had defeated France; she could now send experienced troops to America. But a new kind of leader was rising to the top of the American forces. It included men like Jacob Brown, Winfield Scott, and Andrew Jackson—skilled military men who filled their soldiers with a new fighting spirit.

Proof of this spirit came in July, 1814, in the region around Niagara. Led by Brown and Scott, the Americans won a battle on the banks of the Chippewa River. Scott's men fought especially well. Because of a scarcity of blue cloth, they wore gray uniforms. In their honor, gray uniforms were adopted for the military cadets at West Point.

Scott and Brown pursued the British to Lundy's Lane in Ontario, a mile and a half from Niagara Falls. About 2,600 Americans opposed an enemy force of 4,500 in a battle that stung the British badly. Both Scott and Brown were wounded that day—and, no wonder, for at times the lines were not separated by more than eight or ten paces.

To honor General Scott's men, their uniforms were later adopted by West Point.

The air blazed with shells and rockets. Scott later said that "though both armies suffered greatly, the enemy suffered most." Yet the Americans were not able to push forward after this victory, and within a few weeks British veterans were marching to invade the United States by way of Lake Champlain. Here Commodore Thomas Mc-Donough, commanding the American fleet on the lake, drove them off.

England acted swiftly to take the pressure off Canada. A British expedition reached Chesapeake Bay in mid-August with instructions to destroy the American fleet and capture Washington and Baltimore. A force of militia, regulars, and sailors, thrown together at the last minute, was brushed aside by the British at nearby Bladensburg, Maryland. With the enemy so near, the nation's capital was in an uproar.

319

"May God protect us!" wrote Dolly Madison, the President's wife, as the British approached the capital on August 24. "Two messengers, covered with dust, come to bid me fly . . . a wagon has been procured, and I have had it filled with plate and the most valuable portable articles, belonging to the house. Whether it will reach its destination, the 'Bank of Maryland,' or fall into the hands of British soldiery, events must determine. Our kind friend, Mr. Carroll, has come to hasten my departure, and [is] in a very bad humor with me, because I insist on waiting until the large picture of General Washington is secured, and it requires to be unscrewed from the wall. This process was found too tedious for these perilous moments. I have ordered the frame to be broken, and the canvas taken out. It is done!"

Luckily, Dolly escaped the British invaders. For the inhabitants of the capital, wrote a British soldier, "this was a night of terror." Arriving at the White House, he found the table set for forty guests. The soldiers ate the food and drank the wine, and then burned the executive mansion.

The streets were jammed with a fleeing mob—soldiers and congressmen, men, women and children. Horses raced wildly between carts loaded down with household furniture. The wooden bridge across the Potomac trembled under their weight, then was ordered knocked down after the President reached the safety of the opposite shore.

The British turned next toward Baltimore. They did not attack the city until September 13, when British men-of-war pointed their heavy guns at Fort McHenry, which guarded Baltimore. Aboard one of the vessels was Francis Scott Key, a Washington lawyer. He was trying to arrange the release of a friend who had been captured by the British. Later he recalled the scene:

"The heavens aglow were a seething sea

Dolly Madison saved what she could when she fled from the British attack on Washington.

of flame, and the waters of the harbor, lashed into an angry sea by the vibrations, the *Minden* rode and tossed as though in a tempest. It is recorded that the houses in the city of Baltimore, two miles distant, were shaken to their foundations. Above the tempestuous roar, intermingled with its hubbub and confusion, were heard the shrieks and groans of the dying and wounded. But alas! they were from the direction of the fort. What did it mean? For over an hour the pandemonium reigned.

Suddenly it ceased—all was quiet, not a shot fired or sound heard, a death-like stillness prevailed, as the darkness of night resumed its sway. The awful stillness and suspense were unbearable. . . ."

THE NATIONAL ANTHEM

Francis Scott Key looked toward the fort, where by daylight he had seen the flag bravely waving. Had it been pulled down? He waited anxiously through long hours until through smoke in "the dawn's early light" he saw the fort and the flag. Yes, the flag was still there! On the back of a letter he scribbled lines of poetry to express his joy:

> 'Tis the Star-Spangled Banner,
> Oh! long may it wave,
> O'er the land of the free
> and the home of the brave.

Copies of the poem, struck off as a handbill, were snatched up by the people of Baltimore. A musician, Ferdinand Durang, adapted the words to an old English tune, *Anacreon in Heaven,* and the new song—today our national anthem—was sung all over the country.

Although the British expedition remained in Chesapeake Bay, it did not try to invade Baltimore. Yet Madison was in a desperate situation. The government had neither the money nor the popular support to carry on the war much longer.

New England still talked secession. By the summer of 1814, New England believed that the Federal government would soon collapse. Delegates were invited to Hartford, Connecticut, to consider the question of forming an independent confederation. They met secretly for three weeks, but decided not to take the fatal step of secession.

At sea, the United States met other setbacks. Her frigates were bottled up within harbors so that they could not fight, and even the *Constitution* was driven off the

seas. Yet despite all these discouragements—deadlock along the Canadian border, the burning of Washington, revolt in New England, the overwhelming of the navy—the War of 1812 ended with a triumph. The reason for this triumph was a man who had been born in a log cabin in the Waxhaw settlement between North and South Carolina on March 15, 1767. His name was Andrew Jackson.

Watching the attack on Fort McHenry from a British ship, Francis Scott Key was overjoyed to see the American flag still flying and wrote The Star-Spangled Banner.

A few days after Andy's birth, his father died. Andy was educated in an "old-field school," where he mastered the three R's of readin', 'ritin' and 'rithmetic. By the time he was thirteen, his mother and two brothers had died from hardships suffered in the Revolution. He was seized by the British and carried to Camden, South Carolina.

Andy refused to shine the boots of a British officer, who lashed out with his sword. Andy's arm was cut almost to the bone. He never forgave the British, even long years afterward when, as a citizen of Tennessee, he had become governor of the state.

"OLD HICKORY" AT WAR

The War of 1812 gave Andy a chance to pay off his grudge. He was so rugged that his soldiers nicknamed him "Old Hickory." His campaign against the Creeks after the massacre at Fort Mims in 1813 was a good example of his toughness. He marched his raw militia through a wilderness, and, at Horseshoe Bend on the Tallapoosa River, fought a bloody battle that crushed the Creek rebellion.

Later, convinced that the British were using Spanish-held Florida as a base of operations, Andy drove the British out. New England Federalists howled that Andy had acted without governmental authority. They were right—but Andy simply pushed on to the next spot where he could strike at his old foe.

In December the British marched on New Orleans with 12,000 troops led by Sir Edward Pakenham. Jackson managed to reach the city eight days ahead of the enemy. The British maneuvered for position, which gave him a month's time to dig in. Although he was outnumbered two to one, Andy was not worried. Let the British advance in neat columns, if they liked. Andy figured that his frontiersmen could take care of themselves.

The Battle of New Orleans was fought January 8, 1815. Jackson knew at once Sir Edward had made a blunder when he launched simultaneous attacks with two widely separated forces. He went along the lines, telling his Tennesseans and Kentuckians: "Look, boys, take them as they come—wait till you get them in range and then

When Jackson fought the Battle of New Orleans, he did not know the war was over.

give 'em your shot just above the breast-plates." Andy's boys understood this kind of fighting. The British counted 700 killed, 1,400 wounded, 500 captured. American losses were eight killed, thirteen wounded.

Great though the victory at New Orleans was, it came after the war was over. The news had not yet reached New Orleans, but about two weeks before, at Ghent in Belgium, the United States and Britain had signed a treaty of peace. Both nations were thoroughly tired of the war.

So the War of 1812 was over. And when Madison left Washington in 1817 to return to his home in Virginia, the United States already was well on the way toward entering a period in history that would be known as "the era of good feeling." The year before Indiana had been admitted as a state, and the first tariff bill imposing a tax on imports had been passed to protect American industries.

AMERICA ON THE MOVE

Settlers move westward from the eastern seaboard and establish homes along the frontier.

James Monroe, who followed Madison as President, was the third Virginian in succession to occupy the White House. A veteran of the Revolution, he had served at Princeton, Brandywine, Germantown, and Monmouth. His political career was shaped by his warm friendship with Jefferson.

As a member of the Virginia assembly and the Continental Congress, Monroe fought steadily for a policy guaranteeing free navigation of the Mississippi River to the people of the West. He had been a bit-

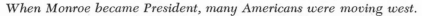

When Monroe became President, many Americans were moving west.

ter opponent of the Federalists in general and of Hamilton in particular.

He served under Washington as envoy to France, then was elected governor of Virginia. He helped to negotiate the Louisiana Purchase for Jefferson, and was appointed minister to England and Spain. He served again both as a member of the Virginia Assembly and as governor, then spent six years in Madison's Cabinet as Secretary of State and one year as Secretary of War.

Monroe took the oath of office in a Washington already largely rebuilt from the ashes left by the British invaders in 1814. He made a tour of the country, visiting New York, Providence, Pawtucket, Boston, Buffalo, and Detroit. He saw with his own eyes how America was changing. Everywhere people were on the move—from farms to new factory towns in New England, from older settlements to vacant lands beyond the Appalachian Mountains.

President James Monroe

They wanted to farm the good land beyond the mountains.

Frontiersmen lived in crude log cabins with few furnishings.

In those days, any region where the frontier existed was called the West. When the Nineteenth Century began, the population of the West was only 386,413, but it grew enormously during the years that followed:

    1810—1,078,315   *1830—3,672,569*
    1820—2,217,474   *1840—6,376,972*

Many things drove people across the mountains. The poor, the restless, the immigrants seeking freedom from tyranny in Europe, New Englanders whose farms were becoming less fertile every year—all welcomed the chance for a new and better life on the cheap land of the wilderness that stretched to the west.

Settlers from New England and the Middle Atlantic states generally traveled the central New York river valley and the Great Lakes, or journeyed by way of western Pennsylvania and the Ohio River, before spilling into Ohio, Indiana, Michigan, and Illinois. Settlers from the South generally used the Cumberland Gap and other mountain passes to reach Kentucky, Tennessee, Mississippi, and Louisiana, or the southern sections of Ohio, Indiana, and Illinois. Each group thus carried its own habits, customs, and beliefs into the wilderness.

Life on the frontier was simple and rough. Home meant a log cabin made tight with clay or mud wedged into the cracks, with shutters or greased paper over the windows, a fireplace of clay and stone, and floors of dirt or puncheons (rough wooden blocks). The early settlers stayed away from the prairies, where there were few building materials and the soil was difficult to plow. They preferred meadows or clearings cut in the forests.

Their furnishings consisted of a table, chairs, a crude bed or two, a spinning wheel, a gun, and an iron crane at the fireplace to hold the pots used in cooking. Men wore deerskin clothes, women dresses of homespun, and youngsters badly fitting hand-me-downs.

The settlers had a constant struggle for food and fuel, and money was scarce. Yet there were gay times, too. Barn-raisings, corn-huskings, and quilting bees brought neighbors together. Preachers traveled through the wilderness, holding "camp meetings." By 1824 there were ninety-eight newspapers in Kentucky, Tennessee, and the old Northwest. Usually these papers took a strong stand on politics, for politics was a serious part of frontier life. Log schoolhouses appeared, and youngsters mastered their three R's or felt the sting of the schoolmaster's switch.

Seeds of Dissension— The Missouri Compromise

The Union tries to exist half slave and half free, but the slavery issue is not solved.

Mississippi joined the Union in 1817, Illinois in 1818, and Alabama in 1819. There were then twenty-two states, evenly divided between those that were in favor of slavery and those that were not. Then Missouri, petitioning Congress for admission to the Union as a slave state, threatened to upset this balance.

Many religious groups, especially the Quakers, had long been troubled by the evil of slavery. Benjamin Lundy, a New Jersey Quaker, became the leader of the antislavery movement. As an apprentice in Virginia, he had seen for himself the cruelty with which slaves often were treated.

In 1815 Lundy moved to Ohio, where he founded the Union Humane Society. Among his early converts was Charles Osborn, whose *Philanthropist* became the first antislavery paper in America. Lundy traveled on foot from place to place, speaking against slavery. Soon he won another ally in Elihu Embree, a Quaker in Tennessee, who began publishing the *Emancipator*.

There were some people who believed that the South could never be persuaded to abolish slavery. In 1816 they organized the American Colonization Society for the pur-

Under the Missouri Compromise, Maine and Missouri were admitted to the Union.

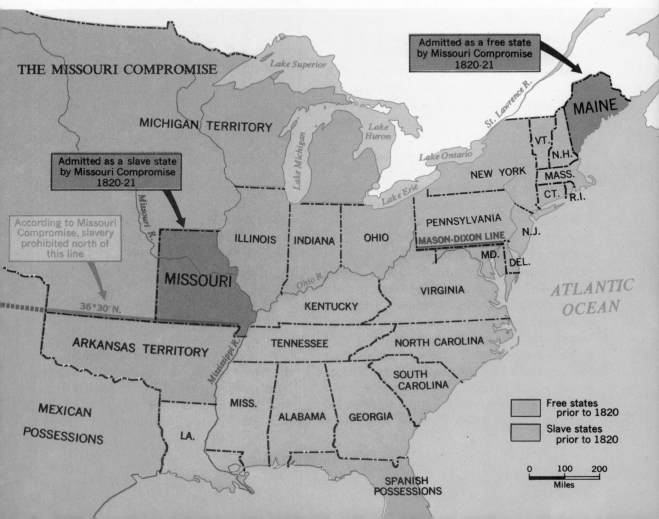

THE MISSOURI COMPROMISE

Admitted as a free state by Missouri Compromise 1820-21

Admitted as a slave state by Missouri Compromise 1820-21

According to Missouri Compromise, slavery prohibited north of this line

Free states prior to 1820

Slave states prior to 1820

pose of sending Negroes back to Africa. By 1820 they had raised the funds to ship back eighty-six Negroes—a drop in an ocean.

But there was no doubt that the antislavery movement would have an enormous effect on the nation. Northern politicians, who had long been seeking a way to stop the rising power of the South, saw that opposition to slavery could be a political weapon. They were soon proved right. In 1819 Congress ruled that slaves "illegally" brought to America—that is, seized without payment to their African rulers—must be returned to Africa. The next year Congress declared slavetrading a form of piracy for which slave traders could be hanged.

The congressional battle over the admission of Missouri as a slave state was a bitter one. The South insisted on "states' rights," while the North shouted that slavery was a sin and slaveholding a crime.

The dispute about Missouri was at last ended by the famous Missouri Compromise. Missouri was admitted as a slave state and Maine as a free state. A line at the parallel of thirty-six degrees, thirty minutes (which runs between Missouri and Arkansas) divided the remainder of the territory acquired through the Louisiana Purchase. All future territories north of this line would be free. Those south of the line could, if they wished, become slave territories. Congressmen shook hands, believing that they had settled the slavery issue.

But the issue did not die that easily. The cause of antislavery kept winning new supporters. The gap between the industrial North and the agricultural South slowly widened. The West, too, was becoming divided. It no longer had a single way of life. The Northwest, where land was cheap and labor scarce, was becoming a region of moderate-sized farms operated by a father and his sons. The Southwest, where cotton, sugar, and tobacco were the chief crops, was becoming a region of large plantations operated by slave labor.

330

THE NATION GROWS AND PROSPERS

Factories rise, transportation is improved, and Monroe warns Europe to stay out of America.

A new development in American life in the Nineteenth Century was the New England factory town. New England's traders and merchants had the money to invest in such enterprises. The many waterfalls in

Slavetrading was legal until 1820, when Congress declared it a form of piracy.

the rivers supplied cheap power to run the machines. Rows of company-owned houses sprang up near the mills to give shelter to the workers. Farm girls, who had learned spinning and weaving at home, were especially needed. Dwellings were provided for them, with house-mothers to look after their personal welfare. Libraries and programs of education and entertainment were set up.

Cotton and woolen textiles were not the only American products. The country was rich in iron ore, and all kinds of metal articles now came from American factories —stoves, steam engines, pipes, beams.

The New England factory town was just one sign of how the North was changing. Another was the flags on the ships that anchored in its ports. America had begun to trade around the world, bringing in tea from China, coffee from Brazil, sugar from Cuba, cocoa from Central America, wines from Madeira and the Canaries. The *Savannah*, partly powered by steam, crossed 331

Many New England factory towns were built near a waterfall which could supply power to run the machines. The workers lived in houses built nearby.

the Atlantic in 1819. Whaling vessels roamed the seas, and by mid-century, 680 such ships set out in a single year to reap a profit from sperm oil and whalebone.

Since 1807, when Robert Fulton's *Clermont* had made a successful voyage up the Hudson, river travel had changed. At Pittsburgh, in 1811, Nicholas J. Roosevelt launched the *New Orleans.* The following year this craft chugged down the Mississippi to the port for which she was named. The age of steamboats had begun, and soon steamboats were crossing the Great Lakes.

Men of imagination talked excitedly of what it would mean to the nation if roads and canals could be built to connect the rivers and lakes. Under the leadership of Governor De Witt Clinton, New York acted while others talked. On July 4, 1817, work began on the building of the Erie Canal. Many people laughed at the canal, calling it "Clinton's Big Ditch." But some eight years later it was finished. The canal was four feet deep, twenty-eight feet wide at the bottom, and forty feet at the top. It crossed New York for a distance of 350 miles. Extending from Buffalo on Lake Erie to Albany on the Hudson River, it linked inland America with the sea. Within twenty years, a boat passed through its important locks every seventeen minutes. About 25,000 "canawlers"—men, women and boys—were employed moving its traffic and feeding the passengers who traveled up and down the canal. Five years after it had opened, Cleveland's population had jumped 400 per cent, Detroit's 300 per cent.

Other states quickly followed New York's example. Pennsylvania built the Portage Railroad, a combined canal and railroad route, to connect Philadelphia and Pittsburgh. Maryland and Virginia planned a canal from the falls of the Potomac to the Ohio River. New Jersey constructed two cross-state canals, and Ohio also built two canal systems. Still other canals were built in Indiana and Illinois.

333

The Erie Canal, running from Buffalo to the Hudson River, was opened in 1825. It helped make New York a major trade center, for goods bound for the West could be shipped up the Hudson and through the canal more cheaply than by any other route.

When on an October day in 1825 the Erie Canal was opened, James Monroe had already ended his second term as President. The Missouri Compromise, the coming of the factory town in New England, and the construction of the Erie Canal had been tremendous events during his eight years in the White House, but Monroe's name would live on for another accomplishment.

THE MONROE DOCTRINE

In his annual message to Congress on December 2, 1823, Monroe stated that North and South America no longer were open for colonization by any foreign power. Should any nation attempt such colonization, the United States would consider its own peace and safety endangered. If any European power should interfere with the independence of governments in North, Central, and South America, the United States would look upon such interference as an unfriendly act. This policy became known as the Monroe Doctrine.

The American continents, by the free and independent condition which they have assumed and maintain, are henceforth not to be considered as subjects for future colonization by any European powers. . . . We owe it, therefore, to candor and to the amicable relations existing between the United States and those powers to declare that we should consider any attempt . . . to extend their system to any portion of this hemisphere as dangerous to our peace and safety. . . .

This statement in Monroe's message to Congress became famous as the Monroe Doctrine. It was meant as a warning to such European powers as Spain, Russia, and France.

A HARDHEADED NEW ENGLANDER

John Quincy Adams becomes President, but is unable to get his program through Congress.

Many persons in Washington said that the real author of the Monroe Doctrine was not the President but John Quincy Adams, his Secretary of State. The son of old John Adams, who as a child had watched the Battle of Bunker Hill, John Quincy Adams had grown up knowing such patriots as Washington, Franklin, and Jefferson. He had traveled with his family on diplomatic missions to Europe before graduating from Harvard and entering the profession of law. He was every inch an Adams—hardheaded, sharp-tongued, quick-witted.

Under Washington, Adams was minister to Holland and Portugal. He served a term in the Massachusetts legislature, and then was elected to the United States Senate. He supported the Louisiana Purchase and the embargo against England and France in the crisis leading to the War of 1812. Madison sent him on diplomatic missions to Russia and England.

As Monroe's Secretary of State, John Quincy Adams became widely known. He arranged the treaty by which Spain ceded Florida to the United States in 1819, and set the boundary between Mexico and Louisiana along the Sabine and Red Rivers, the upper Arkansas, the crest of the Rocky Mountains and the forty-second parallel. He was a candidate for President in 1824, but a strong field opposed him, including tough old Andrew Jackson, the hero of New Orleans. The electoral vote gave ninety-nine to Jackson, eighty-four to Adams, forty-one to William H. Crawford (who

President John Quincy Adams

Henry Clay

Yet even to his own party Adams was a problem. The politicians of his day believed in the "spoils system"—that is, in rewarding their supporters with government jobs and favors. "To the victor belongs the spoils," they said. But Adams refused to play that game. He would not remove men from public office simply because they belonged to a different political party.

Meanwhile, Jackson's popularity grew. Maybe the bankers, the brokers, the contractors, the speculators and the "commercial interests" hated "Old Hickory," but plain people liked his courage and his down-to-earth manner. He seemed to be one of them. In 1829 he was elected President over Adams by an electoral vote of 178 to 83.

"KING ANDREW I"

South Carolina's attempt to choose which Federal laws it will obey is put down by Federal troops.

President Andrew Jackson came to the White House a sad and lonely man, for a few weeks after his election his beloved wife Rachel had died. He believed in the "spoils system" and immediately began to rid the government of his enemies. His opponents howled that he was trying to become "King Andrew I."

Attacks upon the character of the wife of his Secretary of War brought out another trait in Jackson—his chivalry toward women. He refused to believe the gossips. His Cabinet, which did believe them, resigned, and he appointed another Cabinet. His opponents called it a "kitchen Cabinet," held together by love of the "spoils system" and hatred for Adams and Clay.

When Jackson came to the presidency, he inherited the tariff of 1828. Southern-

had served as Monroe's Secretary of the Treasury), and thirty-seven to Henry Clay, the Speaker of the House. No candidate received a sufficient majority. When the election went to the House of Representatives, Clay supported Adams, assuring his election.

Clay became Adams' Secretary of State, and Jackson mistakenly believed there had been a deal between the two men. He watched with satisfaction as Congress turned down bills Adams wanted—bills to build Federal highways and canals, a national university, and Federal weather stations. The country was lining up behind two new political groups, the Whigs and the Democrats. The Whigs supported Adams' program for internal improvements, a national bank, and a high tariff. The Democrats loved Jackson and called all of Adams' measures unconstitutional.

ers believed it was unfair to them and called it the "tariff of abominations." They began to use the dangerous word "nullification," which meant the refusal by a state to recognize or enforce a Federal law. Robert Young Hayne, a senator from South Carolina, addressed the Senate on the nature of the Union and the right of a state to "nullify."

Then Daniel Webster of Massachusetts took the floor. In his reply to Hayne he spoke of the Union, of American nationality as a precious heritage, and of faith in national government. He said:

Andrew Jackson was devoted to his wife, Rachel. Her death, just before he became President, was a great blow to him.

339

"It is to the Union we owe our safety at home and our consideration and dignity abroad. It is to that Union that we are chiefly indebted for whatever makes us most proud of our country. That Union we reached only by the discipline of our virtue in the severe school of adversity. It had its origin in the necessities of disordered finance, prostrate commerce, and ruined credit. Under its benign influence these great interests immediately awoke us from the dead, and sprang forth with newness of life. Every year of its duration has teemed with fresh proofs of its utility and its blessings, and although our territory has stretched out wider and wider, and our population spread farther and farther, they have not outrun its protection or its benefits. It has been to us all a copious fountain of national, social and personal happiness. ... Liberty and Union, now and forever, one and inseparable."

In a famous speech in the Senate, Daniel Webster denied that states had the right to choose which Federal laws they would obey.

David Farragut

"Black Dan" Webster was a great orator, and his speech became famous. But when the tariff law of 1832 included many levies that Southerners found objectionable, a convention in South Carolina on November 24 declared the tariffs of both 1828 and 1832 "null and void." Should the Federal government try to enforce these revenue laws, the convention warned, South Carolina would secede from the Union.

Jackson acted swiftly. A naval force under David Farragut was ordered to Charleston harbor and General Winfield Scott's troops prepared to march into South Carolina. Even a large number of Southern people approved Jackson's stand, and South Carolina backed down.

In a crisis over the banks, Jackson proved how little he knew about money and banking. His attack on the national bank, which had grown steadily stronger since its re-establishment in 1817, brought on one of the stormiest periods of his years in the White House. His opponents tried to limit his power of veto and his right to make appointments. Willing to believe any wild charge against an enemy, Jackson saw himself as "the champion of the people" fighting against the wicked bankers. Unhappily, he won. Public funds were deposited in state banks—Jackson's "pet banks," they were called—and they printed paper money that flooded the country as prices skyrocketed.

341

"REMEMBER THE ALAMO"

American settlers in Texas proclaim independence from Mexico, and show willingness to fight for it.

During Jackson's eight years in the White House, Arkansas and Michigan became states in the Union. The first railroads began operation, and Cyrus McCormick invented his harvesting machine, the reaper. The printing presses developed by Richard Hoe made possible the publication of the first penny newspaper in America.

The Cherokees were moved from their old homeland of northwestern Georgia into the Indian Territory (Oklahoma) and southeastern Kansas, the Seminoles were defeated in Florida, and the Black Hawk War ended the Indians' dreams of remaining on the Iowa prairies. Fur trappers penetrated the Far West, discovering new routes across deserts, plains, and mountains to the shores of the Pacific. In 1836, William Holmes McGuffey, a clergyman, lecturer, and college president, published the first of *McGuffey's Eclectic Readers*, which in time would be read by more than 100,000,000 American boys and girls.

Texas seethed with unrest. The leaders of American colonization in this region were two Connecticut Yankees, Moses Austin and his son Stephen. In 1821, after Mexico had broken away from Spain, Stephen persuaded the new Mexican landlords of Texas to encourage a colony of fighting Americans who would protect the territory if Spain tried to win it back. Land was granted on the Brazos River. It would be tax free for seven years if the Americans would become citizens of Mexico and adopt the Catholic religion. Later, the Mexican government invited Americans to settle in all of the Texas territory on the same conditions.

By 1827, about 12,000 Americans—most of them Southern cotton growers who brought their slaves—had settled in Texas. The Mexicans soon were quarreling with the Americans. To stop the flood of settlers, the Mexican government passed laws abolishing slavery and prohibiting the impor-

The traveling circus was a favorite entertainment during the 1800's.

tation of slaves. Few Americans had kept their promise to become Catholics, and the Mexicans charged them with bad faith. Heavy taxes were levied against the American "intruders."

TEXAS REVOLTS

The most explosive force in this dangerous situation was the rise to power of General Antonio Lopez de Santa Anna. Through various acts this fierce Mexican dictator made clear that he wanted to drive Americans out of Texas. By 1835, the region was in rebellion against Mexico, and in March of the following year Texas declared its independence.

A new Texan army captured San Antonio from General Cos, a brother-in-law of Santa Anna. With a force of many thousands, Santa Anna set out to retake the city. Only a small garrison of Americans had been left to defend San Antonio. They knew they were no match for Santa Anna, but they holed up in the Alamo, an old Spanish mission, and defied the Mexican troops to drive them out.

The defenders of the Alamo, under William Barret Travis, numbered 187. They were a hard-bitten lot—hardy frontiersmen like the old Tennessee Indian fighter Davy Crockett, and Jim Bowie, who

General Antonio Lopez de Santa Anna 343

Next page: *Defending the Alamo.*

Davy Crockett

As the Mexicans approached San Antonio in late February, Crockett wrote cheerfully in his diary: "We are up and doing and as lively as Dutch cheese in the dog days." Next morning Santa Anna's troops appeared. Within the Alamo, Travis and his boys raised the flag of the Lone Star Republic. When Santa Anna demanded that the Alamo surrender unconditionally, Travis answered by firing a cannon ball. In a letter addressed "To the People of Texas," Travis explained his position:

"I shall never surrender or retreat. I am determined to sustain myself as long as possible and die like a soldier who never forgets what is due to his own honor and that of his country. VICTORY OR DEATH."

had given his name to a heavy-bladed sheath knife designed to be thrown at its target. "If there is anything in the world particularly worth living for," Crockett once said, "it is freedom." Men like Travis and Bowie agreed. They tightened their belts and waited for Santa Anna and his legions to storm the Alamo.

General Sam Houston

Jim Bowie

For thirteen days, from February 23 until March 6, Santa Anna besieged the Alamo. Food began running low and, peering over the walls, the Alamo's defenders could see that every day Santa Anna received new recruits for a final assault. On March 4, 1836, Mexican guns rained shot

The defenders of the Alamo fought to the last man.

upon the Alamo. The next day Crockett wrote the last entry in his diary: "Pop, pop, pop! Bom, bom, bom! throughout the day. No time for memorandums now. Go ahead! Liberty and independence forever!"

The defenders of the Alamo all perished. But the Texan army, under tough Sam Houston, had been given the time to gather its forces for a showdown fight with Santa Anna. That battle came along the banks of the San Jacinto River on April 21. To the cry of "Remember the Alamo," Sam Houston's Texans crushed the Mexicans.

PANIC, POLITICS, AND WAR

Van Buren and Tyler each have a stormy term as President, and then Polk is elected and goes to war with Mexico.

Andrew Jackson would have been more than happy to welcome Texas into the Union. But 1836 was an election year and he was anxious to have his own hand-picked candidate, Martin Van Buren, follow him into the White House. The steadily rising antislavery feeling in the North made the annexation of a slave territory like Texas too much of a political bombshell.

The son of a thrifty Dutch tavern keeper from Kinderhook, New York, Van Buren had begun his law career at the age of sixteen. "The Red Fox of Kinderhook," as he was called, was a state senator and the state's attorney general. He was elected to the United States Senate, resigned during his second term to become governor of New

President Martin Van Buren

347

The Panic of 1837 destroyed the savings of millions of people.

York, and then was appointed Secretary of State in Jackson's Cabinet. With Jackson's support, he easily won the presidential election.

Van Buren strolled the streets of Washington in snuff-colored coat, orange cravat, pearl-gray vest, white duck trousers and morocco shoes. He had not been President long when disaster struck. He had Jack-son's foolish banking policies to thank for the Panic of 1837. On May 10, banks in New York City closed; two days later banks in Philadelphia shut their doors. Quickly the panic spread across the country as other banks became unable to meet the demand for payments on their notes in gold and silver.

Stores and factories went out of business,

It was not until 1843 that prosperity returned to the country.

farmers could not sell their produce, and plantation owners could find no market for their cotton. The unemployed roamed the streets.

Van Buren acted sensibly by establishing an independent national treasury. He acted sensibly, too, in settling a Canadian border dispute which saw British troops invading American soil and burning a ship at her dock in Schlosser, New York. This affair could have easily flamed into serious trouble except for Van Buren's firmness and tact. But the people only remembered the hardships they had suffered, and one term was all they wanted of Van Buren.

At last the Whigs had Jackson on the run. Shouting "Tippecanoe and Tyler Too," they swept William Henry Harrison into

349

the White House by an electoral college vote of 234 to sixty. But thirty days after taking office Harrison died of pneumonia.

Now for the first time a Vice-President stepped into the highest office in the land. To make the situation more ticklish, the Whigs had put John Tyler on the ticket only to attract the support of other "turn-coat Democrats." Tyler was not the kind of President that New Englanders wanted.

TYLER AS PRESIDENT

Called "Turncoat Tyler" by his enemies and "Honest John" by his friends, Tyler moved into the White House. He had served in the House and the Senate and as governor of Virginia, and his best known trait was putting conscience before politics. Sometimes he seemed to talk on both sides of an issue—as, for example, when he opposed both slavery and any restriction on the extension of slavery. He argued that the wider the area over which slavery was spread the sooner it would disappear.

Kentucky's Henry Clay, a leading Whig, distrusted him from the start. The old issue of the national bank, which Clay supported and Tyler opposed as unconstitutional, gave the pair the chance to bring their

President William Henry Harrison

feud into the open. Twice Clay forced bills in favor of the national bank through Congress. Twice Tyler vetoed them.

Washington rarely had known such times. Every member of Tyler's Cabinet resigned with the exception of Daniel Webster. An angry mob stormed the White House lawn, hurled stones and insults at the President,

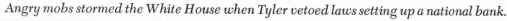

Angry mobs stormed the White House when Tyler vetoed laws setting up a national bank.

President John Tyler

rebellious Senate refused to ratify the treaty. But a new voice was heard when James K. Polk, the Democratic nominee for President in 1844, spoke out strongly in support of annexation.

Tyler was the first man to reach the presidency through the death of another, the first to be threatened with impeachment, and the first President to be married in the White House. Polk was unique, too: he was the first "dark horse" candidate to win the presidency. For seven ballots at their nominating convention at Baltimore in 1844 the Democrats were unable to choose between Martin Van Buren and Lewis Cass of Michigan. Then, to break the deadlock, the little known Polk was nominated to oppose Henry Clay, the Whig candidate.

The chief issue of the campaign was the annexation of Texas. Clay hedged on this question and so managed to reassure neither side. Polk took a firm stand and carried the electoral vote 175 to 105.

THE MEXICAN WAR

Born in Mecklenburg County, North Carolina, and raised in Tennessee, Polk was called by admirers the "Napoleon of the Stump." Election to the Tennessee House of Representatives, the United States Congress and the governorship of Tennessee were offices to which this gift of oratory carried him. He was so devoted a Jackson man that he was sometimes tagged "Young Hickory." That nickname won him few friends with the Whigs, or with Northerners who were dead set against seeing slavery spread.

Cries of "Yankee robbers" rang throughout Mexico over the annexation of Texas. With Polk's inauguration, the Mexican minister broke off diplomatic relations and returned home. A special emissary that Polk sent to Mexico was not even received by the angry government. Troops under General Zachary Taylor were ordered to occupy the region between the Nueces and Rio Grande

and broke windows. A resolution in the House calling for Tyler's impeachment was defeated when Democrats united with Whigs to vote it down.

The annexation of Texas raised another storm. Tyler stood with the South in favor of annexation and concluded a treaty for that purpose with the young republic. A

351

President James K. Polk

Rivers, and warships were stationed off Vera Cruz.

Those close to Polk realized that he was looking for any excuse to declare war on Mexico. On April 25, 1846, Mexican soldiers, crossing the Rio Grande, clashed with a detachment of Taylor's troops. "American blood has been shed on American soil," Polk said, and on May 13 Congress declared war.

"OLD ROUGH AND READY"

In the Mexican War, General Zachary Taylor wins the fame that will carry him to the presidency.

The Whigs protested violently, declaring that "Polk's war" had been started "unnecessarily and unconstitutionally." A young congressman from Illinois named Abraham Lincoln won the nickname of "Spot" for his resolution demanding that Polk identify the exact spot where American blood had been shed. "Let him answer with *facts*, and not with arguments," Lincoln said.

A member of Polk's own party, David Wilmot of Pennsylvania, believed the President was a puppet controlled by the slave interests. He suggested the "Wilmot Proviso" that in any territory acquired through the Mexican War "neither slavery nor involuntary servitude shall ever exist . . . except for crime, whereof the party shall first be duly convicted."

Wilmot attached his "proviso" to many bills that came before Congress. Lincoln remembered voting for it more than forty times. The Democrats doggedly beat down the Wilmot Proviso, but each time it failed to pass, its defeat was like sprinkling salt on the wounds of the antislavery members of Congress.

Polk's worries at home were almost secondary compared to the growing jealousy he felt toward General Zachary Taylor. "Old Rough and Ready," soldiers called Taylor, admiring his style as a fighter. A son of Colonel Richard Taylor, a hero of the Revolution, "Old Rough and Ready" had fought Indians in Indiana, the old Northwest, and Florida. Now, outnumbered at least two to one, he led his army against the Mexican forces under General Mariano Arista. As the Americans approached Fort Brown—and the first battle of the war—officers urged Taylor to wait for reinforcements.

"I shall go to Fort Brown or stay in my shoes," Taylor answered.

Western men knew what Taylor meant. The moment had come "to do or die." Taylor hit the Mexicans at dawn. He pushed through dense tangles of thorn bushes (called chaparral), flung back the Mexicans, snatched blazing cannon from the hands of Arista's gunners, and marched in triumph to Fort Brown. He lost 49 men; the Mexicans lost 1,000.

Taylor then invaded northern Mexico,

General Zachary Taylor

and by September 28 he had captured Monterrey. Here he agreed to an armistice while he rested his weary army, but Polk ordered him to move on. Reinforced, Taylor pressed forward. By the year's end he practically controlled northeastern Mexico.

"Old Rough and Ready's" conquests made him a national hero. This gave Polk much to think about. Taylor was a Whig, and unless Polk was careful the general would be a winner at the next presidential election. So Polk wanted a new general to win his war in Mexico, but the only logical man, Winfield Scott, also was a Whig. Polk toyed with the idea of sending a political friend like Senator Thomas Hart Benton of Missouri to take command, but he knew that Congress would never allow it.

Volunteers for the war were coming in slowly. To give Scott an army, Polk reduced Taylor's army from 10,000 to 5,000. The wily Santa Anna, capturing the dispatches that ordered this cut of Taylor's forces, leaped at his chance. As soon as "Old Rough and Ready's" veterans had departed to join Scott, Santa Anna struck at the remaining troops in the Battle of Buena Vista on February 22, 1847.

From a rise overlooking the battlefield, Zachary Taylor calmly directed his army at the Battle of Buena Vista. By getting his troops and his cannon to the right place at the right time, Taylor managed to defeat Santa Anna.

General Winfield Scott

Taylor took the attack calmly. He knew his boys and they knew him. No general on earth could excel Taylor in giving commands so crisply, so clearly. He watched as the fury of the combat mounted, getting his troops and his cannon to the right place at the right moment. Bit by bit, he cut Santa Anna's army to pieces, and the Mexicans retreated to defend their capital, Mexico City. Taylor's popularity increased with every dispatch of victory. Much against his will, Polk had made a future President.

TWO GENERALS

But Winfield Scott fought no less brilliantly than Taylor. A young lieutenant named Ulysses S. Grant, who fought under both Taylor and Scott, understood the difference between these two generals:

"General Taylor never wore a uniform, but dressed himself entirely for comfort. He moved about the field in which he was operating to see through his own eyes the situation. Often he would be without staff officers, and when he was accompanied by them there was no proscribed order in which they followed. He was very much given to sit his horse side-ways—with both feet on one side—particularly on the battlefield.

"General Scott was the reverse in all these particulars. He always used all the uniform prescribed or allowed by law when he inspected his lines; word would be sent to all division and brigade commanders in advance, notifying them of the hour when the commanding general might be expected. This was done so that all the army might be under arms to salute their chief as he passed. On these occasions he wore his dress uniform, cocked hat, aiguillettes [loops of braided cord on a uniform], sabre and spurs. His staff proper, besides all officers constructively on his staff—engineers, inspectors, quartermasters, etc.—that could be spared—followed, also in uniform and in prescribed order."

In less than twenty years Grant himself was to be called one of the greatest generals of the century, and it would be no secret that he had modeled himself on Taylor rather than on Scott. Yet for all Scott's showiness—he was called "Old Fuss and Feathers"—the old hero of Chippewa and Lundy's Lane had much to teach Grant, just as he had much to teach another young lieutenant on his staff, a brilliant officer named Robert E. Lee.

MEXICO CITY FALLS

Approaching Vera Cruz by sea, Scott captured the city on March 29, 1847, after a siege of less than three weeks. He pushed through the valley of Mexico, won three battles, then stormed Chapultepec, a fortress guarding the western approach to Mexico City. On September 14, 1847, he rode into Mexico City as the conqueror of "the Halls of Montezuma."

THE WINNING OF CALIFORNIA

Americans in California revolt and more territory is added to the United States.

In 1854, the year that James Polk became President, California was still part of Mexico. Here lived the *ranchero,* in comfortable houses built of sun-dried adobe brick. The *ranchero* had helped bring about better government in the territory. But the governors that Mexico sent into California were neither wise nor able. Their mistakes stirred up a spirit of revolt.

American interest in California had begun in the 1820's, when an agent for a Boston firm learned much about the California coast while searching for the sea otter. Soon Yankee traders and whalers in the North

Fur companies set up trading posts throughout the frontier country.

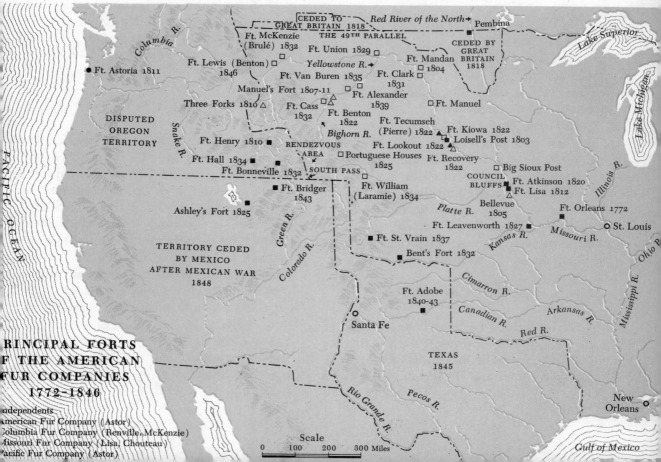

PRINCIPAL FORTS
OF THE AMERICAN
FUR COMPANIES
1772-1846

Independents
American Fur Company (Astor)
Columbia Fur Company (Renville, McKenzie)
Missouri Fur Company (Lisa, Chouteau)
Pacific Fur Company (Astor)

Kit Carson

Pacific made regular calls at California's seacoast towns.

Fur trappers, crossing the high Sierras, descended into the Sacramento and San Joaquin valleys—men like Jedediah Strong Smith, who discovered the Great Salt Desert, and James Ohio Pattie, who brought the first smallpox vaccine into California. Later, three expeditions by Captain John C. Frémont and his famous guide, Kit Carson, greatly added to the knowledge of the rich natural resources of California. And in his book *Two Years Before the Mast*, Richard Henry Dana told of the exciting life along the California coast.

THE CALIFORNIA REPUBLIC

By 1845 there were perhaps 700 American settlers in California. Increasingly they disliked the highhandedness of the Mexican governors, and at Sonoma in 1846 a band of Yankee rebels ousted the Mexican military commander and seized the *presidio* [fort]. William B. Ide, a farmer, ripped down the Mexican flag, raising in its place a homespun banner with a star, a bear and the two words, "California Republic."

Texas had not been Polk's only objective when he asked Congress to declare war on Mexico. So, as Taylor marched on the Rio Grande, another American force under Stephen W. Kearny left Fort Leavenworth, on the Missouri, to invade New Mexico and California. Kearny marched his army down the Santa Fe Trail. By mid-August of 1846, he had captured the settlement of Santa Fe without a struggle. Cocky and self-confident, he divided his army and set off for California with 300 cavalrymen.

Crossing the Rio Grande at Albuquerque, Kearny met Kit Carson, who carried dispatches from Frémont to Washington reporting that California already had been successfully conquered. When Frémont had learned that the United States was at war with Mexico, he had become a busy warrior in his own right. By midsummer of 1847 the Stars and Stripes had been hoisted at Monterey, San Francisco, Sutter's Fort, and Sonoma.

KEARNY PUSHES FORWARD

Kearny, listening to Kit Carson, decided on a quick push into California. Sending back his wagons and 200 of his men—and with Carson for a guide—Kearny traveled by pack mule to the Gila River along a trail that even the animals found difficult to cross. The general followed the river through a crisscross of mountain ranges, camped beside giant cactus plants, visited with the peaceful Pimas and Coco Maricopa Indians, and pushed on to the junction of the Gila and Colorado Rivers.

But Kearny's heroic march was far from ended. Another 150 discouraging miles stretched ahead. Kearny's little army desperately needed water and native Californians attacked his battered columns. A relief expedition, sent out from San Diego, finally rescued those who survived. By January 13, 1848, Kearny and Frémont completed the conquest of California.

The Mexican War had fulfilled most of Polk's dreams. A peace treaty was signed in the little town of Guadalupe Hidalgo on February 2, 1848. In exchange for $15,000-000 in cash and claims, the United States secured the Rio Grande as its boundary. Mexico gave up its claims to the territory that today includes California, Texas, Arizona, New Mexico, Utah, Nevada, and part of Colorado. In a later treaty with Mexico, signed December 30, 1853, the United States purchased the land between the Gila River and the present Mexican border. This was known as the Gadsden Purchase.

OVER THE OREGON TRAIL

England disputes America over the Oregon Territory.

Before Polk left the White House, the Pacific coastline of the United States would extend from San Diego, California, to Puget Sound, Washington. Some of the territory was gained in the Mexican War, the rest through settlement of a dispute with Great Britain over boundaries in the Oregon country.

The "Oregon Question" really dated from 1792 when an American explorer named Robert Gray discovered the Columbia River. Following international practice, the United States claimed sovereignty over the river's valley and watershed as well as over the nearby coast.

England disputed the claim, declaring that Gray's voyage had been commercial and not official. Then in 1805 the Lewis and Clark expedition, reaching the Pacific,

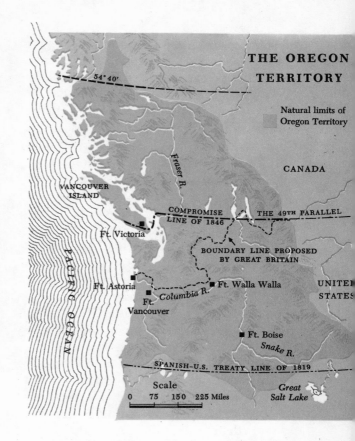

THE OREGON TERRITORY

Natural limits of Oregon Territory

strengthened America's claim to the Oregon country. Six years later fur trappers working for John Jacob Astor established Astoria, an American settlement and trading post, on the site where Lewis and Clark had spent a winter.

The War of 1812 gave the British the chance to force American competitors out of the Oregon fur trade. Although the treaty of Ghent restored Astoria to American ownership, the rivalry between the two nations in this territory was far from ended. In 1818 and 1828, agreements were reached that the country "westward of the Stony Mountains" should be open to the "vessels, subjects and citizens" of both nations. But a strong-willed Englishman, John McLoughlin, was in control of the Hudson's Bay Company, and it looked as though the British would win the race for settlement.

Then something unexpected happened. Jason Lee reached Fort Vancouver in 1834 and settled in the Willamette Valley—the 359 first of the missionaries to enter the Oregon country. Marcus Whitman and Henry Spalding arrived two years later, establishing a mission near Fort Walla Walla. In 1839, under Fathers Blanchet and Demers, a Roman Catholic mission was set up at Cowlitz, in the present state of Washington. Letters, speeches and pamphlets by these missionaries—and Washington Irving's *Astoria*, a novel romanticizing the expedition of Astor's fur trappers in 1811—helped to spread "the Oregon fever."

"The Great Migration" in 1843 brought about 900 settlers to the Oregon country. In another three years there were some 6,000 American settlers in the territory, outnumbering the 1,000 British. The Americans fought their way over the Oregon Trail. Starting at the Platte River in Nebraska, they drove their wagons up the North Platte into Wyoming. Ten miles a day was a good pace as they followed the Sweetwater River in Wyoming, where they caught their first glimpse of the snow-capped Rockies. Weeks later they struggled down the western slope of the continent.

At times a wagon train, lumbering over the Oregon Trail, would number 1,000 persons. The sight was like that of a whole town on the move with all its wagons, animals, and household furnishings. At the head of the column rode the pilot, who knew the country and the Indians. A band of from ten to fifteen men rode off each morning in search of buffalo herds. Four watches at night, from eight o'clock in the evening to four in the morning, guarded the party while it rested.

FIFTY-FOUR FORTY OR FIGHT!

When the Democrats nominated Polk for President, one of their campaign slogans was "Fifty-four Forty or Fight." This meant that they wanted the territorial dispute with Britain settled at the latitude of fifty-four degrees, forty minutes or they would go to war. But Polk wisely avoided a conflict with England by settling upon the forty-ninth parallel of latitude, the present boundary.

Polk had much to show for his four years in the White House. The disputes

The Oregon Trail began in Nebraska, crossed the Rockies, and went into Oregon.

over Texas and Oregon had been settled, and Wisconsin and Iowa had joined the Union. The United States Naval Academy had been founded at Annapolis, adhesive postage stamps had been used for the first time, and inventions like Elias Howe's sewing machine and new types of farm equipment were making life easier in rural areas. In 1846 came the beginning of the great Mormon migration into Utah, and steamboats traveled the Mississippi. In Barnum's Museum in New York City, people gazed with wonder at oddities assembled from around the world.

Polk wished only one term as President, and the Democratic nomination in 1848 went to a hero of the western men, Lewis Cass. But what Polk most feared came to pass. The Whigs had found a winner in Zachary Taylor.

FILLMORE SUCCEEDS TAYLOR

In 1848, gold was discovered in California. Within twelve months 260,000 Americans had journeyed by land and sea into the territory. The "Forty-Niners" gave colorful names like Git-Up-and-Git and Lazy Man's Canyon to their mining towns. A few struck it rich, attracting the gamblers, the desperadoes, and the dance-hall girls. Bands of citizens known as vigilantes enforced what law there was by a rope slung over the branch of a tree.

Yet not for long could Congress forget the rumble of thunder that echoed through its halls. Friends and foes of slavery were forming like rival armies as the debates began on whether the territory acquired from Mexico should be free or slave.

No one could question where President Taylor stood. He was squarely for the Union and against giving in to the South. His Vice-President, Millard Fillmore, took the opposite position. Within sixteen months after taking office "Old Rough and Ready" ran a high fever, resulting from overexposure to the sun during a Fourth of July celebration. Five days later, on July 9, 1850, he was dead. So Fillmore, the friend of the South, became President and America began its march toward Civil War.

Wagon trains with as many as 1,000 persons traveled it during its peak years.

THE NEXT VOLUME IN THIS SERIES

VOLUME

5

THE CIVIL WAR

*Volume V, The Civil War, tells of the
deepening distrust between North and South over the slavery
question, and of how that distrust
finally developed into civil war.
It is the story of how the once united states
broke into two warring camps, of the battles
fought and the blood spilled before they rejoined.
Both sides had their heroes,
both made their blunders, but for four years,
brother fought against brother in a cruel war that ended at
Appomattox Court House with the South almost destroyed.
Shortly thereafter, a President who wanted
to help the South recover was
killed by an assassin's bullet.
This book covers the years 1850 to 1865.*